Gabby-
you are
gorgeous!
Follow your
heart! Love,
Dana

SOLO IN THE SPOTLIGHT

A practical guide to stepping out of your shadows of doubt and fear and into the light of success in all areas of your life.

DALE SMITH THOMAS

Solo in the Spotlight
Dale Smith Thomas

Copyright © 2004

ISBN: 0-9760177-0-9

Cover Photo: Todd Killen
Cover Design: Bill Kersey, KerseyGraphics
Printing: Vaughan Printing, Nashville

CONTENTS

APPLAUSE TO THE FOLLOWING SPOTLIGHT DREAM TEAM

~ To my team that has always encouraged me to perform in my spotlight I can never thank you enough.

~ To my husband, Rob, your presence in my life has given me wings to fly to destinations beyond my dreams. Your love and belief in me is one of my greatest gifts.

~ To my son, Nick, you are the greatest example of performing "solo in the spotlight." Your courage inspires me daily.

~ To my personal "dream team": Kathryn, Dana, Darcy, Shelley, Tom, Larry, Jane and Joe. You have challenged me, pushed me, inspired me and loved me. I love you so much!

~ To all of you on my Motivational Monday Team thank you for consistently checking on my progress as I have worked on this book. Your presence in my life is invaluable.

~ To my parents and my brother for loving me unconditionally and for supporting me as I have lived my dreams I will eternally be grateful.

~ To Genie who is the greatest designer I have ever known.

~ And finally to God I dedicate this book for all the blessings I have had in my amazing life.

This book is dedicated to everyone that dares to step out of the shadows of their life and dance in their personal spotlight of success.

INTRODUCTION

I want to first say, "Wow, it's done!" For those of you who have followed my work through the years you know that this has truly been a journey for me. I have written and re-written this book so many times. I sent it to a great editor only to realize that in doing so that I was walking away from exactly what I wanted to share. I write like I talk and I always wanted this book to be a conversation between you and me. However, I realized an editor can't do that, only I can. I am sure deep down it has been the fear that has kept me returning to rewrite and rewrite. Well, the rewrites have stopped and I am taking the Leap of Faith to give you my heart and soul through the written word.

No, this book isn't going to be perfectly written but you can be sure that my heart and soul has been laid out on the line to you. This book is about the lessons I have learned and yes it is a little autobiographical. You will travel with me back in time as I share some of the stories and people that have shaped my life and therefore lead me to be here right now.

Why have I titled this book Solo in the Spotlight? It is because that has been my life's journey and I think the journey of so many people. This book is meant to challenge you to step out of whatever shadow has been holding you back and it's to encourage you to step into the full spotlight of your life. The good and the bad news is that only YOU can decide what your true spotlight is for you! It took me a long time to find that place. But, I truly rejoice that although it took me well into my 30's to find it, I did find it and so can you.

As you pick up this book I really challenge you to make it work for you. I know that some of the ideas I have may not work for everyone that reads it, but take what works for you and apply it. It doesn't matter how old you are, what stage of life you are in at this present moment there is something here for you. I believe that you have been lead here for a reason. I don't believe it's an accident that you are holding this book in your hands right now. There are answers here for you and for the questions that you have in your life. I ask you to open your heart, your soul and your mind and be ready for some amazing insight that will not come from me but will come from within you. The stories I share, the lessons I will share, will guide you to find your own personal spotlight.

My journey into the spotlight began on the dirt roads of Mississippi. I was born and raised on a farm 10 miles outside of Eupora, Mississippi. This tiny little town of 2,000 people was where it all began for me. I have to honestly admit that growing up in that little town I never dreamed that one day you would be reading words I had written. I never dreamed that one day I would be the one standing in the spotlight on stages around the world or sitting in a spotlight in a television studio. The road that let me here has been filled will lessons and learning.

This book is about you; I'll share my personal experiences and some experiences of others in hope that our stories and our lives will reach your heart and your soul. It is my belief that success, advancement, and personal progress comes when we learn to step out of shadows of fear and doubt and dare to be Solo in the Spotlight. Dreams, goals, and fulfillment can only come from our personal solo performance. We can have our supporters cheering us from the audience or even standing behind the curtain but our real performances in life are "solo" performances. It's up to us to maximize our talents and use them to the best of our ability. It is my desire that this message will help you face your fears and doubts and that daily you will work toward finding your true spotlight and that when you walk off the stage of life that you will have given a standing ovation performance. Thank you for making this journey with me.

With Love and Encouragement,
Dale Smith Thomas

"We all have many gifts that we've never opened. It's time to open some of yours. Find your wings !!"

DAN ZADRA

CHAPTER ONE

Identifying Shadows and Recognizing Light

You may be asking exactly what I mean when I say we all need to step out of the shadows of doubt and stand *Solo in the Spotlight.* You may not have a desire to be in a literal spotlight but this book is about life principles that can motivate you and help take you to a new level in your life. I believe that there is a spotlight for all of us. It's our place to shine and express our greatest gifts. I believe that we have to push ourselves to step out of the comfort zone and the shadows of our fear and find our personal spotlight. Shadows and spotlights are complete opposites but one does not exist without the other. We would never understand light without darkness. We would never understand faith without fear. We would never truly understand victory without defeat. It is the dark times, the shadows, that teach us about light. This book is to help you identify those shadows in your life and encourage you to step boldly into your spotlight of success.

Have you ever noticed that with just a small amount of light, the darkness starts to disappear? Light a match, or a candle and what do you notice? The darkness disappears. Many times the darkness that surrounds us is our fear. Our fears keep us tied to the shadows of doubt and unbelief. Our fear of what we will find in those shadows keep us from taking the risks we need to take so we can become what we were created to be. But, there is exciting and liberating news for all of us. With just a small bit of light, those dark shadows of fear will disintegrate. Remember when you were a small child and you thought you saw things in the dark and they scared you. They really didn't exist. You realized it was your imagination when you turned on the light. Light always overcomes darkness, but it is up to us to turn on the light inside our souls and release the darkness we face. We have to turn the light on our fears and watch them disappear. When you turn on the light, the light in your soul, you will find your spotlight. Finding that light—your spotlight—is what this book is all about.

I believe shadows are those places where we run and hide when we don't want to face our truth, our gifts or ourselves. It's the place we believe is the only safe place to be. But to live our lives to the fullest, we have to take a leap of faith and walk out of the darkness to search for the light. Only you can begin the search for finding your place, your destiny, and your spotlight. This is your personal journey and one that no one else can make for you.

SHADOWS AND LIGHT

What is this spotlight that I keep referring to? It's the place where you can shine, regardless of what others think about you. Stop and think for a moment how you feel about people in the actual spotlight. How do you describe them? How do you feel about them? We seem fascinated with famous people. For years, I looked at entertainers, actors, and other famous people and thought they were the "lucky" ones.

Because they are "successful", we think sometimes think they are happy and know who they really are. Of course, as we all know that is not always true. Often we read about their lives and we realize that are often unhappy and don't have a clue about themselves. They aren't happy about who they are or what they are doing. They haven't found their true spotlight. However, we do read stories of famous people who love their chosen profession and it radiates from their soul. The spotlight I am describing is that place inside yourself, in your soul, where the light shines from within. The energy from you just glows. It's a place where you feel warm and happy with who you are and what you are doing with your life. It's being all you are supposed to be regardless of who supports you. It's taking complete control and ownership and responsibility of the gifts that God gave you. It's being responsible to you for you!

WIRED TO LIFE

When you stand in your own personal spotlight, it's as if you have an earpiece and you are getting directions from another source, the source of your soul. I am sure you have noticed entertainers who wear earpieces when they perform. All live television personalities work with an earpiece. It allows the show's producer to talk to them while they are on the air. Just a few years ago I was a guest co-host of a morning show. I remember the first day the producer gave me my earpiece. It was strange to hear someone talking in my ear when I didn't expect it. I think I actually screamed when he first spoke to me because I wasn't expecting it!

I think in our day-to-day lives we have access to our own personal earpiece that allows us to hear what our heart and soul is saying, but most of us never listen to these voices. We ignore the direction we feel we are receiving. You can call it your inner voice, your intuition, or whatever name works for you. I call it my earpiece to God, my Higher Power. He gives me inspiration and direction I need in my life.

I believe we often turn off the earpiece and ignore what our heart and soul is saying to us. Instead, we listen to the negative messages coming from ourselves and others. We listen to those who tell us why we "can't" do something or why our dreams will never be realized. We tell ourselves we are "too old", " not educated enough" , "not talented enough", "not good looking enough" and the list goes on. Instead of listening to the positive messages coming from our inner voice, our Higher Power, we turn our earpiece over to fear and doubt. I wonder why we give so much more "airtime" to negative thoughts, and very little time to the positive messages in life. It's as if we think negative messages are real and positive messages are unreal. I truly believe the more we allow negative messages to enter our minds and souls, the harder it is to recognize the positive messages in our lives. They poison our souls and our dreams. Those negative thoughts become magnets for more negative thoughts. What we focus on gets bigger.

I am sure you have had an experience where you felt you were being led to do something. Sometimes it is very hard for us to stop and follow the direction from within when we are getting so much unsolicited advice from the outside. When you step out of the shadows that bind you to someone else's opinion, someone else's approval, you can step into the spotlight with your arms open wide. You can let your soul scream for joy, shout, and celebrate. You are free to be who you want to be.

YOUR CIRCLE OF LIGHT

I believe that our lives are a journey. We are constantly seeking a place where we can be happy from within. When you find that place where you are happy in your own skin, confident in your choices, and confident in following your inner guide, you have found your spotlight. Regardless of what situation you may face, you have a place you can go in your mind and soul; a place inside yourself where you feel safe. When you can be comfortable, happy and accepting of yourself regardless of the critics in your life, you have found YOUR spotlight! Some days it will be a huge, bright circle of light that surrounds you. Those are the days when you feel supported, loved and encouraged by everyone in your world. However, there will be other days when the light is so small you can barely see it. Those are the days when it's important to remember that you are valuable; you have the ability to win. You can trust yourself with the decisions you have made about your life. Even though the light around you feels small, the light is still there.

FIRST STEPS TOWARD BEING FREE

My journey has taken me from a rural upbringing on those dusty, gravel roads of Mississippi to where I am today. I remember what I now consider my first solo journey. I was in first grade. I had never been away from my mother in the six short years of my life. I had never spent a night away from my Mom or even spent time with a baby sitter. I was her shadow and she was mine. I did not have any idea what it meant to do something by myself.

I can still remember how I felt that first day of school as I climbed on that big yellow bus, I felt fear and absolute terror. Mr. Edwards, a kind, gray haired man, greeted me from his seat behind that huge steering wheel. Tears rolled down my face as I tried to find a seat. From my reaction you would have thought my parents were sending me away for the rest of my life, not just for a few hours! I was afraid of the unknown, of being alone, and of not being accepted. Of course, my feelings were not based in reality. It was just first grade, but I was still afraid.

Regardless of how ridiculous my fears of first grade seem now, it wasn't ridiculous then. It was real. Our perceptions are our reality even if they are ridiculous. I was six years old and terrified as I faced my first solo journey. It took me two weeks to get comfortable with my first big adventure. I must admit my change of heart was motivated by my Mom threatening to get a tree switch and spank me if I didn't stop crying and get on the bus! Isn't it amazing how one fear can instantly replace another? I made the transition into first grade with the help of a new friend, Anne Middleton. She was as terrified and as fearful as me. Even at six, it was nice to know I wasn't alone. We all need to feel that way once in a while.

As you have figured out, I survived first grade. I survived my first solo flight out of the first shadow. Each phase of our life is a new journey and brings new challenges and new fears. Have you ever had an experience similar to my first solo journey? Can you remember your very first solo journey, or any solo journey? Can you remember a time when you had to step out of a shadow or a place of comfort into the unknown? Do you remember a time you had to step into a spotlight or a time you were forced to be there?

Maybe you eased into the experience without fear or hesitation, or maybe you faced it like I did, shaking all over! Regardless of how we face these experiences, we all have those times when we must walk alone. We have them our entire lives. I hope you will let this book be a journey back into those places, but also a catalyst for the many spotlights in your future.

My journey began with fears and tears. As I reflect on those days,

I think of the many journeys we face alone. We are born, we go to kindergarten, first grade, we graduate, we go to college, we have that first day on a new job, new co-workers, or starting a new life with a new partner. We have so many beginnings and so many times we must stand alone. We must learn to embrace ourselves and know that the strength we need and the power we possess totally comes from within. When we have that personal "earpiece" linked to our Higher Power, we are never really alone. We may have to take the step, make the leap, get on the path, but when we realize we are never really alone, we begin to move forward with a new sense of purpose.

Throughout our lives we have to take small steps to take us to the bigger events of our lives. We learn to ride a bike with training wheels before we tackle the "big" bike, we learn to crawl before we learn to walk, and we learn to walk before we run. All the experiences in our lives are constructed with small things that will take us to a higher level. When it is our turn to stand alone in the spotlight of life, all of the small spotlight appearances throughout our lives will have prepared us for the moment. Doing the small stuff prepares us for the big stuff. We set small goals before we reach out for the big ones.

I meet so many people in my travels that are frustrated because things are not happening in their lives as fast as they think it should. It's part of our "I want it now" culture. It's hard for us to be patient and pay our dues. Because of our impatience, I know we miss so many treasures in our lives by not living today as we are working toward tomorrow. Living in the present moment is the only way to prepare for the future. It is the journey that teaches us, molds us, and inspires us to be all that we are created to be. These small, solo steps teach us, but many times we miss the lesson because we are complaining that our lives are not progressing fast enough.

SUCCESS, IT'S YOUR CHOICE

I have studied and observed successful people for many years. I have studied their lives, their habits, their way of thinking, the way they speak to themselves and to others. And I've discovered something incredible. These people are no different than you and me except for one thing: They have learned a formula for success. They have learned and applied a new set of skills to create the results they want in their lives. How do they do it? They are students of life. They learned from their mistakes and situations that were difficult. They realize every experience can be a learning experience. I believe successful people learn from other successful people by observing what they do, what they say and how they live their lives. They realize that all information is learned skills and acquired knowledge. The people that I consider "successful" are not just presidents of companies or superstars. They are mothers and fathers who are raising great children, they are small business owners, they are schoolteachers, farmers, and salesmen. Success is an attitude, a spirit and a way of life. It is deciding to give your life your 100% best effort. No, it's not easy; it takes practice and work. It is being willing to learn something new about yourself each day. It's learning that to be successful, you have to *choose* success

IDENTIFYING YOUR SHADOWS AND LIGHT

The only way for us to move to the next level in our lives is to identify where we are and what we can learn from our past experiences. We need to look honestly at the shadows in our lives that are holding us back. We need to take an inventory and face our fears. Take the time right now to think about these questions. Remember you are reading this book for a reason. Listen to yourself, discover your answers and write them down. This exercise will only be effective if you do the work. If you want to take your life to a new level, you have to be a student of success and do the work from within. Start looking for any shadows of doubt that have been holding you back and begin moving toward your success spotlight!

What do you consider your first solo journey?

How did it make you feel? Did you approach it with excitement or fear?

What fears have you carried with you from childhood?

What is your definition of success?

What areas of life have you had success and climbed into your spotlight? How did it make you feel?

What shadows or fears do you need to face right now?

What is your inner guide or High Power telling you to do?

What goal do you need to pursue?

SPOTLIGHT QUOTE

"The only way to overcome darkness is to flood it with light." The only way to overcome your fears is step up with action. Action is the light to cure your fear."
(author unknown)

"When we walk to the edge of all the light we have and take the step into the darkness of the unknown, we must believe that one of two things will happen. There will be something solid for us to stand on, or we will be taught to fly."

PATRICK OVERTON

CHAPTER
TWO

Taking The Risk
of Being You!

SELF ESTEEM AND RISK

Before we talk about self-esteem or self-acceptance, we should define what it is. In the dictionary, self-esteem is defined as how much a person likes, accepts, and respects himself overall as a person. When you have a healthy self-esteem, you know who you are. You are proud of yourself and totally comfortable in your own skin. Your belief and attitude about yourself should never be influenced by others. You are a valuable person. It doesn't change with circumstances or the opinions of others.

What are some characteristics of individuals who have low self esteem or high self esteem? Here they are !

Characteristics of low self-esteem:
You demean your own talents.
You feel that others do not value you.
You feel powerless.
You are easily influenced by others.
You express a narrow band of emotions.
You avoid situations that provoke anxiety.
You become defensive and easily frustrated.
You blame others for your own weaknesses.

Characteristics of high self-esteem:
You act independently.
You assume responsibility for your actions.
You are proud of your accomplishments.
You approach new challenges with enthusiasm.
You show a broad range of emotions.
You tolerate frustration well.
You are capable of influencing others.

I provided this list for you because it is something I struggled with for so many years. I heard people talk about self-esteem, but I truly didn't understand it. I hope you really looked at the list and

22

asked yourself how you feel about your self-esteem. It's a good idea to take inventory and see how you truly feel about yourself. If you identify that you have low self-esteem then you can begin to work on changing it. If your self-esteem is high then you can continue to build it.

BATTLE OF SELF

As I mentioned earlier, my young life started with fear, shyness and low self-esteem. I didn't know who I was. I didn't believe in myself and my opinion of myself changed with the opinion of others. I was tragically shy during my elementary and junior high school years.

Do we ever get over those feelings from our youth? I don't think so. I have asked thousands of people questions about their self-esteem and it seems that many fight the battle of poor self-esteem, doubt and fear throughout their lives. I think as we grow and develop from within, we find courage and new ways to continue to fight those old messages of doubt and unbelief. I have found that taking risks and trying something new has helped build my self-esteem. When we take risks, we step out of our shadow of comfort and push ourselves to be more. When we do, it gives us a sense of accomplishment and the courage to take even more risks.

Some people are born with "no fear" tattooed on every page of their life; they are born risk-takers. I know these people exist because I gave birth to one. My son, Nick Thomas, has always been a risk taker. From the time he was able to walk he surprised me by what he could do. Because of my past problems with fear and doubt, I quickly realized I had to be cautious on how I directed Nick. Since most fear is learned fear, I didn't want to instill any unnecessary fear in him. I wanted him to be cautious but also confident. Nick grew up having a great sense of self. Now, as a teenager, he isn't afraid to take risks. He skies black diamond slopes, he races motorcycles, he races four wheelers and anything else that has speed. I admire the "risk taker" in him but as his mother it some-times scares me half to death.

As I look back at my early years, I NEVER took risks. I honest-ly smile at myself now and it feels good to laugh at what a real chick-en I was in every sense of the word. I drifted through elementary and junior high school wondering why I was so alone. It never crossed my mind that I was alone because I wasn't reaching out to other people. I believed I was strange and different. I was convinced that no one else felt the way I did. I felt like I was on the outside looking in and that no one understood what I was feeling.

After being painfully shy my first few years of elementary school, something special happened to me in fifth grade. That someone spe-cial was my teacher, Mrs. White. She actually noticed me, a scared, big-eyed little girl wearing homemade clothes and living in her own shadow. Mrs. White made a huge impression on me because she encouraged me and made me feel important. How did she encour-age me? First, she noticed me. I think we all just want to be noticed. We need to feel that we are not invisible. Mrs. White believed in me. She gently encouraged me to get over my shyness and showed me it was OK to speak up for myself. I know she gave me the first glimpse of my true self. Mrs. White, with her beautiful gray hair and warm smile, began to coax me out of that cave of self–doubt I had created and been hiding in for years.

TELL THEM NOW

A few years ago I went home to visit my family and to visit my grandmother at the local nursing home. As my mom and I were walking toward my grandmother's room, she said, "Did you know that Mrs. White is here, too?" I hadn't thought of Mrs. White in a very long time. Mom shared with me about her illness. It was hard to believe that this woman who had made such a lasting impression on my life was now just down the hall from my grandmother.

I decided to stop in and see her and I was completely overwhelmed. The woman I had admired so much was unable to speak or even move. But there on the nightstand was a photo of the woman I remembered so many years ago. As I stroked her hair, big tears rolled down my face. I leaned over and quietly told her what she had meant to me. I softly explained who I was and what a huge difference she had made in my life. When I asked her if she knew who I was, she moved briefly. Even though she didn't open her eyes or speak, I am going to believe that she understood.

As I walked out of her room, I wondered why I had waited so long to tell her how important she was to me. What did Mrs. White really do for me? She simply noticed me in a room full of chatty, wiggly fifth graders. She gave me her attention. I wasn't the smartest, funniest, or the nicest student in her class. But I was the student who felt invisible. She saw that and with her sweet smile and loving spirit she helped me begin to feel worthwhile. I will never forget how her acceptance made me feel. I believe she helped me begin to move out of that lonely world of self-doubt I had created at such an early age.

We all have people in our lives that encouraged us to move out of that dark place, but many times they leave our lives before our journey is complete. I know Mrs. White would be proud of me now. I encourage you to find those people who made an impact on your life. Let them know what they did for you.

My journey out of the shadows really began with the help of Mrs. White. I truly wish she could see that the little girl, who wouldn't make eye contact, wouldn't talk to anyone, is now traveling the world talking for a living.

Do you have a Mrs. White or someone like her who has helped you on your journey? Let them know! Is there someone in your life that needs to be encouraged? Is there someone in your life that needs you to take notice of them? Look at those around you and let them know how valuable they are. Tell them today.

SMALL STEPS

Although Mrs. White had a huge impact on me in elementary school, my biggest journey from the shadows to the spotlight came in high school. The move from the shadows into the spotlight was forced on me; it was not my first choice. Honestly, it was out of necessity.

Throughout junior high school I did not have the courage to join any clubs or audition for any groups. However, when I went to high school, I finally had a goal. I wanted to be a Eupora High School Cheerleader. As I was writing this book I really asked myself why that was so important to me at that time. I remember watching the cheerleaders and in my eyes, they seemed so happy, accepted and "popular". I wanted to feel that way, too. In my school, cheerleaders were elected by the student body. I thought if people liked me enough to vote for me to be a cheerleader, then I must be OK. My attempt to join the squad was my search for self-worth and acceptance. I was looking for votes to prove I had value.

It does seem odd that I wanted to be a cheerleader when I was petrified to talk to people or even speak out loud. In fact, when my teachers would call on me to answer a question, I would almost be physically sick. I was so afraid I would be wrong, so desperately afraid of being rejected. Nevertheless, I still wanted to get into the big ring and run for cheerleader; something that could lead to major rejection! And it did. I was not elected. I found out I lost the election by one vote. I remember how devastated I felt. One vote! How could I be so close yet so far away? I didn't have the skills at that time to see the loss as a learning experience. It is always hard to look at the tough times and learn something. I only understood the pain I felt. All the negative things I thought about myself seemed to be true.

MOTIVATED BY PAIN

In my youthful eyes, a miracle occurred that summer. One of the cheerleaders decided to drop out and I was asked to join the squad. I remember the day I found out! It was a mixed bag of joy and doubt. On one hand, I didn't win on my own; someone had dropped out. On the other hand, I was ecstatic. I was a cheerleader! It seems so silly now that being a cheerleader was such a BIG DEAL to me, but I was 15 and it was HUGE deal. I achieved my goal. I want to remind you that whatever goal you have, don't trivialize it. If it's something you believe in and want it is NEVER trivial even if the world may think it is! I believe you have been given that desire for a reason. I don't believe we are ever given a dream that we aren't capable of fulfilling.

I will NEVER forget the day the head cheerleader said she had to talk to me. She sat me down and said, " Dale, I have to tell you that if you don't start talking to people and talking to the football players, we are going to have to let you go from the squad." I was crushed. I had barely reached my goal of becoming a cheerleader, and now she was telling me I might be kicked off the squad. The very idea that a cheerleader would have to talk and be social. Come on, I thought it was about being accepted, being popular, wearing cute cheerleader outfits and doing cheers in front of the crowd. Why should I have to talk to the football players, what did they have to do with this? Why did I have to talk to anyone for that matter?

At that moment I had a decision to make. I had to decide between pain and pleasure. Many of the decisions we make throughout our lives are a decision between pain and pleasure. The pain of being kicked off the cheerleading squad was much more painful to me than having to talk to any football players or students. So I decided to stay, stepped around my shyness and began talking to everyone. I even made a point to learn the game of football so I could talk to the players about the game. I knew more about the game than most of the guys did (I still do). Thankfully, it worked. I followed the rules and they let me stay! Today I tell people I learned to talk in the late 70's and I haven't stopped talking since!!

It's comical that I now travel the world talking to strangers! That one experience forced me to be more assertive and helped me begin to develop my spotlight esteem. It didn't happen because I wised up, learned how to set goals or suddenly learned how to develop myself personally. I was motivated by fear. This was my first real accomplishment; I had to stay on that squad. I took a very challenging situation and learned from it. I even went on to be head cheerleader my senior year.

Taking risks and taking small steps—even if we are forced to take them—are all part of finding out who we are so we can step into our spotlight. I never dreamed in high school that one day I would be sharing my message with people from around the world. I didn't know my life experiences were teaching me lessons that would change my life.

Take the risk and discover who you are, regardless of your age or where you are in your life. If I could talk to you right now, could you tell me your greatest gifts? If I asked you what makes you unique, could you tell me? If I asked you what makes you really happy, could you tell me? If I asked you to give me a 30 second commercial on "you", could you do it?

It's easy to look at other people and see all of their great qualities. It's so much harder to look at ourselves and see the same greatness. Take time and look inside yourself right now. Take the risk to get quiet so you can listen to your heart and soul. Take time to find the gifts that belong in your spotlight.

Success Work

What are your best qualities?

What risks have you taken in your life that you are proud of?

What did you learn by taking those risks?

Who do you know that is a great risk taker? What qualities do they have?

Name three people you know who have a strong sense of who they are and show it daily. Did you put yourself on that list? If not, why not?

What experience forced you out of your comfort zone? Can you see the lessons you learned from the experience?

Write a 30 second commercial on yourself. What are your product benefits?

SPOTLIGHT QUOTE

"When the defining moment comes, either you define the moment or the moment defines you."
(From the movie, Tin Cup)

"If you are distressed by anything external, the pain is not due to the thing itself but to your own estimate of it; and this you have the power to revoke at any moment."

MARCUS AURELIUS

CHAPTER
THREE

---

*The Lessons of Pain
and Pleasure*

PAIN OR PLEASURE

When I was a cheerleader in high school, I didn't know I was learning one of the most important principles of my life. I learned that we will do more to avoid pain than we will do to gain pleasure. Think about that for a minute. We make changes in our lives when we are in pain or trying to avoid pain. Pain is the precursor to change. If you are sitting with your legs underneath you and your leg goes to sleep, you move it when it becomes painful. We make changes in our lives when we are in pain. It was more painful for me to think about NOT being a cheerleader than it was to talk to people.

Who knew the little girl who wouldn't talk to anyone would eventually be talking to everyone? (In fact, my husband wants to know where that girl is now and can we occasionally bring her back!) My manager says just give me a word— any word— and I can talk for a half hour. It has been fun to go back to several class reunions and see my classmates. They are always amazed at how I have changed. They can't believe it is the same person.

And the truth is, it isn't the same person. That old person had to face her fears, change, grow and learn to develop new skills. She learned and developed into someone new. What did I do? I faced my fears, I took a risk and I made the choice to really work hard for something I wanted. Think about a butterfly. It has to break out of its cocoon to become something beautiful. It has to break free to fly. We wrap ourselves in our self-doubt and it becomes our cocoon. No one can break the cocoon from the outside. They can give us suggestions, they can tell us what they see, but we have to break free from the inside out. We must break free to fly!!

When I was young, I had very few people in my life who were willing to talk to me straight about the chains of negativity I had gathered around me. I did have one person who helped me begin to uncover and focus on my positive characteristics. My piano teacher, Cheryl Prewitt. From the first day I walked into her house for my piano lesson she would NOT let me talk about my self-doubt when

I was in her presence. Cheryl was my teacher, my mentor and my friend during my teenage years. She taught me how to play scales and sonatas, but she also taught me important principles that have molded my life.

Cheryl's positive attitude and spirit were confusing to me. She had suffered so much at such a young age and had every reason to be negative about life. At 11, Cheryl was severely injured in a head on car accident. The motor of the car landed in her lap and crushed her left leg. She also went through the windshield and her injuries required 100 stitches in her face. When she was examined by the doctors in my hometown hospital they told her she would probably never walk again. The doctors put her fractured body in a full body cast and told her parents there was nothing more they could do. The bone in her left thigh was so shattered they were uncertain if it would mend. But, Cheryl had the faith of a child. She had been in Sunday School all of her life and she had been taught that God was like her father. She rationalized that since her Daddy wanted her to walk, God did, too. We should never underestimate the simple faith of a child. Over the next few months they watched through x-rays as a cocoon of calcium formed around all of those crushed pieces of bone. When they removed her cast months later, the bone had mended, but her right leg had grown several inches longer than her damaged left leg. She was walking again, but by your standards and mine, she was handicapped.

FOCUS ON POTENTIAL, NOT LIMITATIONS

During the time that Cheryl was struggling with her disability, she did something that truly impressed me. She focused on her abilities, not her disability. She focused on her potential, not her limitations. She focused on what she COULD do not what she couldn't do. I think that is very rare in anyone of any age. Most people faced with that kind of challenge give up. They focus on what is wrong not on what could be. They are ruled by fear and not by faith. Why is it so much easier to see what is wrong with us than it is to see what is right? In the last chapter I asked you to write down your best qualities. Did you do it? Is it easier to write down what you want to change about yourself? Was it easier to point out what is wrong with you, instead of what is right? Are there things in your life you KNOW you need to change? Do you think there are things in your life that others can see that you do not see?

Do you have one person in your life that really knows you and will be honest with you? Do you have the courage to ask them what they think you need to change in your life?

Remember, if you ask the question, you must be ready for the answer. Sometimes we ask people to give us their opinion and then we don't like what they have to say.

I have someone in my life that gets in my face and makes me get real when I want to hide. He makes me mad, he ticks me off, but he pushes me to grow. I may not speak to him for weeks, but when I calm down, I realize that what he said is what I needed to hear. Even now, after years of growth, study and hard work, I still have to fight the old demons of doubt that want to come back and play in my spirit.

What are you afraid of? Is there self-doubt that you need to face? Are there things in your life you need to change before pain forces you to make a change? Are you in a situation you know you need to change but it's just not painful enough yet? Make the change before it becomes too painful.

RECOGNIZE YOUR SHADOWS

If we truly want to grow and maximize our lives, we must learn to recognize our fears, our shadows and use these revelations to move into a more fulfilled life. It may be tough to look into those places we had rather ignore. In order to make lasting changes in our life we must first acknowledge what needs to be changed. My friend

Cheryl faced her disability and her fears with faith. In fact, she told me for years she believed she would be healed of her disability. She just "knew it" would happen. I can promise you that I was very doubtful and many of you may be doubtful as you read these words. It was truly shocking to me that a few years later it did happen. She was miraculously healed and went on to achieve some incredible things I will share with you later. It simply didn't matter if I believed it or if you believe it. The only thing that mattered was that Cheryl believed. She had faith to see with her inner vision. Just like Cheryl, you have to be able to see what you want with your internal vision. We have to face the fears in our lives and fight those fears with unstoppable faith.

FACE YOUR FEAR

If you have read any self-help books, you may have heard author Denis Waitley describe fear as an acronym: false evidence appearing real (FEAR). Most people think they understand what it means until they are faced with fear. Then fear looks too real to us even if it isn't.

When I need to deal with my fear, I look at Nick, my son. He is fearless. Take, for example, skiing. Nick is great on skis; I am NOT! I admit I am not only afraid, I am scared to death. I broke both of my elbows several years ago and the fear of falling and breaking them again keeps me from wanting to go down a mountain at any rate of speed. But, I am good sport and I promised my family that I would give this sport they love a try. On a ski trip several years ago, I went to ski school, learned the basics and finally made it down the bunny hill. I was so proud of myself that Rob, my husband, thought we should videotape my great success. He skied down in front of me to capture this accomplishment on tape; the kids were behind me just in case I didn't make it all the way down. I was doing great until my ski got caught in some powder and I not only fell, I wiped out! In fact Rob called my not so graceful fall a "yard sale" because all my

35

ski stuff was scattered all over the mountain. My skis were gone, my poles were gone, and my sunglasses were gone. I was just lying on my back looking at the sky wondering what I was thinking when I put those skis on my feet. My feet belong in high heels, not in skis. I thought if I lay here long enough, one of those cute boys on the snowmobiles will come and rescue me because they will think I am hurt badly. As I lay there, I was being passed by three year olds. You feel pretty ridiculous at the point. It was at that moment, I heard someone skiing toward me and sliding to a perfect stop. I knew without looking it was Nick. He wondered if I was OK and asked if he could help me up. I told him to go away. I told him I knew if I laid there long enough the ski patrol would eventually come and get me. He laughed and told me to get up and he would help me get down the mountain. I told him I didn't like this and I didn't know how I was going to get to the bottom of the mountain because I was scared of falling again. Nick looked at me and said, "Mom, you are just going to have to face your fear. You have to set a goal and just ski toward that goal. I know you can do it." He continued by saying, "Mom, you know you teach other people to face their fear, now you have to face yours." I was ready to kill him. I told him (lovingly, of course) that I didn't need a motivational speech while I was lying in a foot of snow. He laughed, helped me up and skied down with me, slowly. He was right. I just had to stand up and do it. I had to stop focusing on falling and start focusing on getting down the mountain. I realized I had no choice. If I ever wanted to get those skis off my feet and back into high heels where they belonged, I had to face my fears. Many times when we are faced with fear about the end result then we just have to focus on what we can do at that moment. I had to focus on the two feet in front of me, not the distance down the mountain. Little by little I moved forward and eventually made it to the bottom. It was a true learning experience. I don't have many experiences where I am almost paralyzed with fear but I was that day. It was a lesson I will never forget. I realized that when you are really hit with fear you really don't want to hear the truth, I sure didn't. I wanted the easy way out but my son would not let me take it and I am glad he didn't. I am not a great skier; I doubt I ever will be. But I am not paralyzed with fear any more. I know my limitations and I ski within my level. I even enjoy it. Nick thinks I am still a chicken, but you know what, that's o.k.

Life is like skiing. We may fall, but we have to get back up. You have to push hard, take risks, and sometimes fall on your backside. My friend, author and motivational speaker, Les Brown says it perfectly, "If you can look up, you can get up."

Is there a fear you need to face right now? What shadow of fear are you living in? Is it your career? Is it your closest personal relationships? Is it a talent you have? Are you just standing in the shadows waiting for someone to discover you instead of taking action? Well, you better get guts-to-the-wall honest and realize you have to take control of your thoughts, your fears, your actions and ultimately, your destiny.

JUST GET HONEST

It starts with just being honest. We don't like to admit that we are really afraid. I hated to admit that I was afraid of skiing down the hill when I was being passed on the slope by three year olds.

There are times in our lives we are motivated by pain. There are times we are motivated by fear. There are times we are motivated by someone who is pushing us to move on. And there are times we are motivated by the inner voice that guides us. Instead of being motivated by fear, pain or someone else, we should be our own motivation. We should make changes because we have made the decision to do so. Your past does not have to create your future. Let's learn from our past and create a future that puts us in the spotlight we choose. We have to recognize the shadows that have created us, the fears that have changed us and the doubt that has held us back.

It's time to do some house cleaning, my friends! We don't like to admit what our gifts really are because we don't want to sound arrogant. God put YOU on this planet with special gifts. HE wants you to use them and share them with the world. You can't sit around and just wait for the spotlight to find you. What gifts do you have but you haven't used or developed because of fear or self-doubt? What thoughts instantly come into your mind?

I encourage you to stop and write down your answers. I know those dreams are popping up in your mind like popcorn; don't ignore them. You can push them down but they will continue to rise. Let's bring them up NOW and take that first step. Let's send a message to the shadows and tell them their work is done. We're moving on!

What do you need to change about yourself to be more effective in your life?

What painful experience motivated you? What did you learn from it?

What darkness or fear are you running from?

What unfulfilled dreams, goals, and desires are just waiting for you to dust them off?

What visions and dreams have you placed in the attic of your mind and soul? Are they collecting dust and you can barely recognize them because they are covered with so much self-doubt?

SPOTLIGHT QUOTE

"Faith is daring to put your dream to the test. It is better to try to do something and fail than to try to do nothing and succeed."
Dr. Robert Schuller

"Aim for success, not perfection. Never give up your right to be wrong, because then you will lose the ability to learn new things and move forward with your life. Remember that fear always lurks behind perfectionism. Confronting your fears and allowing yourself the right to be human can, paradoxically, make yourself a happier and more productive person."

DR. DAVID M. BURNS

CHAPTER FOUR

Let Your Lessons Lead You

The lessons and ideas I am sharing come from years of standing in the shadows. I see so many people who seem to be more content to stand in the shadows than to risk stepping out into their own spotlight. They would rather support the star than be the star. There is nothing wrong with being the support person but, many people do so because they are afraid to be in the spotlight themselves. They don't try for the team, or audition for the role, or submit their resume for the job because they are sure they won't get the top spot. I know, because that's what I did. I finally realized you miss all of the shots you never take.

LITTLE FISH, BIG POND

Throughout high school and college, I worked to be in the spotlight. I really wanted to see what it was like to be in that spot. After my experience as a cheerleader in high school, I wanted to be in a lead role once again. I continued to try, but my efforts always seemed to fall short. I was always second place or the one next in line. I allowed myself to become comfortable with being in the shadows. After graduating high school, I attended a very small junior college because I was just too frightened to go to the big state school. I decided it was easier to be a big fish in a little pond. When I say the college was small, I mean small. I graduated with just 11 other students. I don't think I can even call my college a pond; it was more like a mud puddle.

When I arrived at Wood Junior College, my goal was to get involved and get that "spotlight" chance. The high school I had attended did not have a theater department. I was thrilled to find out that theater was a big department at Wood. I had always enjoyed watching actors on stage and in the movies. I had always harbored a secret dream of being on stage; a dream I left hiding in the shadows. When the theater department held auditions for the first play of the year, I didn't hesitate, I auditioned for the lead role. I was a freshman that had never been a play and I was not cast in the lead. I was disappointed but happy that I had been selected for another role. I told myself this was my first play and I should be happy just being part of the show. When the department announced auditions for another show second semester, a dinner theater production, I was ready. I told myself I now had the experience and I wanted the lead role. I worked so hard and just knew that I would be selected. It was the perfect part for me. It had my name written all over it. Only 4 people auditioned for this role so I just knew it was mine.

I couldn't wait to get to the theater the day the roles were posted. As I stood in the dark hallway alone and scanned the list, my heart sank straight to my feet just like a rock sinks to the bottom of my daddy's fishing pond. I was again cast in a minor role; the lead went to someone else. I was devastated. I had heard the quote, "There are no small roles; only small actors," but at that point in time, it didn't mean anything to me.

LET DEFEAT GUIDE YOU

I'll be honest with you, I felt sick when I saw that list. Losing the role to someone else just reinforced my inner belief that I did not deserve to have the lead in anything. Although I had a part, it wasn't what I wanted. Author Sophia Burnham says, "Many people pray and receive the answer to their prayers, but they ignore them or deny them, because the answers didn't come in the form they expected." Trust me I couldn't see that my prayers were being answered at all. This definelty was not the form I was expecting. However, I knew I had a choice. I could let this decision affect my ability to perform in a secondary roll or I could have the right attitude, work hard at the role I was given and prove to the director that I truly was the best person for the job. It seemed that just as I changed my attitude the circumstances suddenly changed also. Within the first week of rehearsal, the girl who was cast in the lead role decided to drop out and I was recast in the role. I was happy, but I felt like I was back in high school. I was chosen because someone dropped out not because I earned it. What kind of pattern was this? I felt like I was second choice and I didn't like the way it felt. I didn't realize that I could only feel like I was second choice if I decided to feel that way. Eleanor Roosevelt said it best when she said, "No one can make us feel inferior without our consent."

I will never forget the first night of play rehearsal. I walked into that bland, small cafeteria and sat down with the other cast members. I am sure I had a twinkle in my eye because I had a surprise for them. Earlier, the director had said that anyone with less than twenty lines needed to have them memorized by the first rehearsal. My bright yellow play book was worn out before the first rehearsal. Although I had more than five hundred lines, I had already memorized every word. I wanted to be completely prepared for the first rehearsal. I felt a real sense of accomplishment when I told the cast I had memorized all of my lines. I could tell by the expressions on their faces that they didn't believe me. But I knew what I had accomplished. I was determined to prove to the director that even though I was second choice, I was a good choice. My hard work also helped me prove to myself that I could do the job. The play was a great success and I knew I was part of that success.

UNUSUAL WAYS

What would have happened if I had taken a negative attitude concerning the play and how I was cast? I would have been miserable and my bad attitude could have kept me from being offered the lead role. Many times our dreams come to us in unusual ways; ways that are not always our first choice. It's up to us to turn them into an advantage. We have to stop asking why things have happened this way, and ask how we can make the best of the situation. Then move on! I think that is worth repeating: We have to stop asking why and ask how and what.

TOUGHEN UP

When things happen that aren't a part of our plan, we have to toughen up, accept what has happened and make plans to move forward. I don't like being tough. It's been a difficult lesson for me to learn. I firmly believe in the old quote that says, "We miss so many opportunities because we are still staring at the door that has been shut." I challenge you to only glance at the door that has slammed in your face, understand the lesson and move on. When something unexpected happen we have to stop asking why it happened and ask, "What is next!" Refuse to dwell on the door that has closed. Learn the lesson and move on.

There are so many stories of people who have been knocked down to only get up again and achieve incredible success. Did you know that Michael Jordan was cut from his Jr. High basketball team? What did Michael do? Did he complain and whine about what had happened to him? Maybe he did, but he also took action. He started practicing his shots more than he had ever practiced before. He dedicated himself to becoming better at his craft! What was the result? He will be remembered as one of the greatest basketball players of all time. I found this quote by Michael Jordan that I really love he said, "I have missed more than 9,000 shots in my career. I have lost almost 300 games. On 26 occasions I have been entrusted to take the game winning shot...and missed. I have failed over and over again in my life. And that is why I succeed."

There are times in our lives we are going to get knocked down, not hit the mark, or not reach the goal. The question is, what will you do then? Will you allow it to teach you and help you grow to achieve an even greater level? I trust you will. Let those "shadow" times encourage you to take action, improve your attitude and your skills and help you reach a level even greater than before!

I believe it's the bumps in the road, and getting thrown a curve that pushes us to grow. So the next time you get thrown a curve in life, remember this quote, "Throw me a curve, make me grow."

What can we do when we face an unexpected, unpleasant situation? Ask yourself questions!

What can I learn from this situation?

How do I move forward from here?

What do I need to change about myself to move forward toward my goals?

How am I letting this situation affect me? Am I sending myself more negative messages?

Where is this lesson leading me?

Is this a lesson that continues to repeat? What am I not learning?

Has can this obstacle be an opportunity?

What do I need to learn about myself from this lesson?

SPOTLIGHT QUOTE
"Those who aren't making mistakes probably aren't making anything."
Samuel Smiles

"The less you speak, the more you will hear"

ALEXANDER SOLSHENITSEN

CHAPTER
FIVE

Listen to Your Guiding Inner Voice

When things happen in our lives that are unexpected and outside of our plan, it is very hard to not listen to the negative voices that wage war in our heart, soul, and spirit. It is easy to listen to the voices that say, "Why did you think that would work out?" or " Who do you think you are?" However, we pay too much attention to the old negative thoughts and messages. Unfortunately, those negative voices usually do not belong to someone else, they are coming from inside of us. We have to learn to balance our listening.

WHAT DO YOU HEAR?

Listening. Why do we have such a hard time with it? I believe listening and trusting are two of the most difficult things we ever try to do. We grow up being told we don't listen and we end up teaching the same thing to our children. Yet, do we really ever teach them how to listen? I don't remember being taught how to listen to someone else or *how* to listen to myself. How many times as a child do you remember being ask this question, "What do you think you should do? What do you feel you should do?" Many times we are told what we should do, and what we should think.

Have we been told so many times "we don't listen" that it has become a self-fulfilling prophecy? Do we really know how to listen? Isn't it *rare* when we meet someone who really listens? We know they aren't just hearing the words but they are listening to the messages of our heart. Have you ever talked to someone while they look over your shoulder and scanned the room? I hate it!! Do you want to continue to share your innermost thoughts and feeling with this person? NO! It makes you feel unimportant and shows that the person isn't interested in you, what you are saying or how you feel. Don't we long for just one person who will truly listen not just to our words, but to the messages in our hearts? When someone we love isn't listening, we feel like they don't really care about us.

LISTEN TO YOUR SOUL

Others may not listen to us, but are we listening to ourselves? Do we really listen to ourselves, to our inner voice, our inner guide? Ralph Waldo Emerson wrote about listening to our inner voice. He said we should go against all voices that are contrary to our inner voice. Emerson said we are most effective when we are listening to that inner voice. I believe our inner guide and soul feels like we do and wonders why we are not listening. We get a thought, a direction, an idea but we won't stop long enough to really listen. We're too busy. We're too angry. We're too tired. We turn a deaf ear to the most important voice that will ever speak to us. We walk away. But, I believe our inner voice continues to whisper to us. I know mine did. One of the hardest things we will ever do is take that leap of faith and ACT on what we believe we are being instructed to do. We question ourselves and often convince ourselves not to act.

Many of the greatest gifts I have received in my life happened because I was brave enough to listen to my heart and follow it. It took me years to learn how, but the good news is it is a skill that can be learned. It is one of the most important skills we can ever learn.

SOUNDS OF SILENCE

What happens to you when you become quiet? Maybe it's been a long time since you just sat in silence and tried to listen to your inner guidance. We seldom just sit and listen to our souls. We drive our cars with the radio blaring. We feel uneasy when a conversation lags and there is silence. Most of us are uncomfortable with silence. I love what Wayne Dyer, author of many self-help books, says about silence, "It's really the space between the notes that makes the music that we enjoy so much. Without the spaces, all you would have is a continuous, noisy note."

I believe everything that has been created begins in silence. When have you just sat in silence, and listened to that voice, the message in your heart? Do you hear your inner voice speaking to you? What do you do when it says something to you? Have you ever noticed that you have conversations with yourself all the time? I recently read *Conversations with God,* a book based on listening. Regardless of what you think about the book, I admire the author for sharing exactly what he was hearing in his soul.

NEVER TOO LATE

Wherever you are in life, it is never too late to begin to listen to what your heart and soul has to say. Each day that we wake up is a new day. We have a chance to make a new start and do something different with our lives. You can begin listening to that voice that speaks to you from within your soul. You can stop ignoring the direction you are given on a daily basis. The voice inside you has been calling you for a long time and is still calling you. Don't turn up the volume in other areas of your life to drown out your inner voice. Don't be too busy to listen. The dream, the goal, the mission you have on this earth will never go away. It will never quit calling you. It will continually say, "Hey, I'm over here. Please pay attention." You can choose not to listen and never fulfill your calling, or you can take a step of faith and not only listen but act!

FOLLOW THE CALL

Have you ever spoken to someone who loves what they do? They often say they were "called" to do the work they do. That is exactly how I feel about my work and life mission. I have heard many people say it, especially those who choose to go into the ministry. I have also heard actors say they felt they were called to do their jobs. What do you mean? I think it means they feel they were put on this earth to do that one thing, whatever it may be. They know exactly what they were put on this earth to do.

I know the greatest gift I can give my son is teach him to listen to his inner voice for guidance. I heard my calling years before I ever followed it. You may be asking what it sounded like or felt like to me. It was just being directed and drawn toward something I loved. I was always drawn toward the stage but I didn't know how to follow that interest. I had no one to guide me. Working on the stage seemed impractical. It was easier to ignore what I was feeling and to stand in the shadows.

JUST BE PRACTICAL

I started taking piano lessons at the age of eight. I had an interest, but I know my parents hoped it would help me overcome my shyness. I enjoyed playing the piano but hated the thought of piano recitals. However, it was the price I had to pay for having the opportunity to continue playing. I can remember the fear I felt when recital time approached. I felt sick and my legs shook so much I could hardly get through my piece. I felt like I wouldn't survive but I did. I found that taking action and working through my fear taught me how to love piano. I continued to train for 14 years.

PLAYING IT SAFE

Because I had this secret desire to perform, I thought music was the only way I could get on the stage. But music wasn't my natural gift; I had to work hard and it frightened me. It wasn't until I went to college that I discovered how much I loved theater. I had found a place where I could be on stage, enjoy it and not be scared to death! I had found a home. Have you ever had a similar experience? It feels like all of the pieces of the puzzle fit. That is how it felt for me. But, even after my experience and success in junior college theater, I still played it safe when I transferred to Mississippi State University. I stopped auditioning for plays because I told myself it wasn't practical. I couldn't use a degree in theater. After all, there weren't any calls for actresses in Webster County! What would I do with a theater or speech degree?

At the time, my negative, very chatty, inner voice was telling me I wasn't pretty enough, smart enough, or wealthy enough to be on the stage. I let the censors, the voice of defeat, take me away from what my heart was guiding me to do. Author Susan Jeffers says, "We have been taught to believe that negative equals realistic and positive equals unrealistic." I knew if I told anyone about my dreams, they would tell me how unrealistic I was being. So, I didn't tell. I didn't even audition while I was at Mississippi State. I let my negative beliefs create my reality. I told myself I had to get a "real" degree so I could get a "real" job. I rationalized that the degree I wanted and loved wasn't "practical". I also told myself I couldn't pursue theater as a hobby because I needed that time to work.

I talked myself out of the one thing that had brought me so much joy.

GOING AGAINST THE GRAIN

So, what did I do? Instead, I pursued a physical education degree. Those of you that know me are probably laughing right now. For those of you that don't know me personally, I am NOT the athletic type. Honestly, the only thing that runs on me is my mouth! The thought of me coaching basketball or any sport is really a stretch and rather comical. I am just not that type of girl. I don't have the shoes! All through college I knew I had made a bad choice but I was too afraid to look inside myself, listen to my heart, and follow through with what my heart was telling me. I majored in physical education because it sounded logical. I rationalized. I told myself teaching was all I could do in my hometown. I struggled to get my degree. I wasn't athletic then and it's pretty much the same today. I can't even describe to you how much I had to struggle to get that degree. My major was heavy in subjects that were very difficult for me. I was totally going against my natural gifts. With determination, hard work and many long hours I finally received my degree and although I don't coach sports today, I am coaching others in life!

RED FLAGS WAVING

Has there ever been a time in your life when you have done something even though red flags were going up and slapping you in the face? Was it a relationship? A job? A career or a college degree? When you look back at the situation, how many times were you right? Most of us have had this type of experience. Why do we do it to ourselves? Why do we ignore the inner voice, the guide, and even the red flags? Is it easier? It was for me. It was easier to play it safe and get the physical education degree than to follow my heart. It never crossed my mind that I could leave Webster County and pursue my dreams elsewhere.

Whatever voice is calling you, I just encourage you to listen and explore the possibilities. No, we can't do everything we dream of doing. I can't be a basketball player or a concert pianist, I don't have the skills. But I encourage you to really listen to your heart and soul. Listen to the voice that is calling you and at least explore what you are hearing.

—— Success Work ——

Do you listen to yourself?

What do you hear?

Name one person that really listens to you. How does it make you feel?

Are you a good listener? If not, why not?

What red flags have you ignored in your life?

Do you have an unspoken dream or calling that has been whispering to you? What is it? Write it down.

Spend twenty to thirty minutes just being quiet and listening. Write down everything you hear or think you hear. Don't question it, just do it.

Listen to yourself. Follow your guide and stop ignoring the red flags. They are red for a reason. It means STOP!!

When you listen to your self- talk is it more positive or negative?

When you listen to the quiet are you comfortable or uncomfortable?   Why?

Shut out the noise of the world at least once a week and just find some quiet. Rest your soul.

SPOTLIGHT QUOTE
"Knowledge speaks, but wisdom listens."
Oliver Wendell Holmes

"Man's main task in life is to give birth to himself, to become what he potentially is. The most important product of his effort is his own personality."

ERICH FROMM, PSYCHOLOGIST

CHAPTER SIX

Wear the Shoe That Fits

Getting my degree in physical education was difficult for me because I was going against the design of my life. I was going against my inner voice. The classes required for this degree were heavy in science and totally went against my natural strengths and gifts. It was frustrating. Have you ever had an experience where you're working hard at something but it feels like it is going against all your natural abilities? Are you working really hard on something in your life right now that isn't working? Stop, look and listen to your heart and not your head. Ask yourself why it is so hard. Ask yourself the tough questions. Many times what seems practical isn't what you should be doing with your life. We KNOW in our heart but our head convinces us it is the right thing to do. We are afraid to trust that inner voice so we wander in directions we aren't meant to go. When we are truly following those special gifts we have been given, it will be like putting on a shoe that fits.

SHOPPING FOR THE RIGHT SHOE

Trust me; shoes are something I know about! I am a shoe freak. I have over two hundred pairs of shoes. These aren't just any shoes; they are high heel shoes. If I find a great shoe for a great price, I buy it even if it's a half size too small. When the shoe is pretty and the price perfect, I convince myself that I can squeeze into that shoe even if it's uncomfortable. The truth is, I can only wear it about five minutes before it starts killing my feet. I believe it's like this in our lives. We try to wear shoes that don't fit. My college advisors told me a degree in physical education was a great fit for me. It made logical sense but it didn't fit the natural design for my life. They meant well and they wanted to help. If anyone had really looked at the areas that I really excelled they would have realized I should have been pursuing a communications degree not a "physical" education degree. We all have well-meaning people in our lives that can give us similar advice, but we have to wear the shoes (the dreams) that fit our lives.

WEAR THE SHOE THAT FITS

Just like Cinderella, the right shoes only fit you. Your dreams, your natural gifts, and talents, only fit you. You can try to force yourself into another shoe, another dream. You can wear it ; you can get by but it doesn't feel comfortable. It hurts, it's stressful, and it's uncomfortable. You become irritated, anxious, and *really* unhappy. Are these types of symptoms showing up in your life? If they are, is it because you are in someone else's spotlight and not your own? I truly believe that when we are doing what we were meant to do, we will love it.

WHEN YOU LOVE IT, IT SHOWS

I mentioned in the last chapter about those individuals in life who know they have found their calling. Have you ever talked to someone that really LOVES what they are doing? Did you notice the energy in their voice? Did they tell you it really didn't seem like work and they would do it for free if they had to? Did they have a radiance around them that was noticeable? Did their eyes just shine? Could you feel the joy? That's how I feel when I talk about what I do. I LOVE it! My husband is in sales and has been for 25 years. He loves it. When he has had a great day, he comes home energized. He loves the strategy, the contact with other people and the challenge. He knows this is where he belongs.

When you hear some of the Hollywood greats interviewed, they talk about how much they LOVE what they do. I am in a profession that scares most people to death. Public speaking is one of the biggest fears people have. It energizes me. I absolutely love it. When I come off the stage, I feel like I glow like a neon light. It doesn't drain me; it inspires me.

WHAT ABOUT YOU?

What about you? Do you really like where you are on a day-to-day basis? What do you say when people ask if you like what you do? Do you tell people you love it or is it just a job to pay the bills to get by? Listen to what you are saying. If what you do makes you feel fulfilled, then you have found your spotlight. If you're unhappy and unfulfilled in your work or life, keep searching! You need to find your spotlight!

I believe if you are unhappy and unfulfilled, it will take its toll on your emotional and physical health. Are you happy where you are? Is it time to begin your search? The giant spotlight is out there searching, going back and forth across the horizon looking for you. It's trying to locate you and to focus in on you. It can't find you because you are hidden behind the curtains of your fears and doubts. You haven't heard your inner voice. If we don't become quiet, we won't have to listen to what our heart and souls are saying.

Do you remember the heavy, dark velvet curtains hanging in your high school auditorium? Imagine yourself being wrapped in those curtains, hiding. It may feel safe, but it is also stifling and dark. It's time to come out from behind the curtain. It's warm and bright in your spotlight. It has energy that will keep you going. Your steps to get there may be slow and it may take you some time to cross out of the shadow into the light, but you must begin now. Today is the day!

DON'T RUN AND HIDE

If you run from your dream, your true spotlight, it will follow you and try to catch you. Your dream will call you! Have you ever watched a singer in the spotlight? Have you noticed that as they move, the spotlight follows them? The same is true for your dream. If you refuse to get quiet, and refuse to listen to your inner voice or your dream, it will follow you until you turn around and face it.

How will you know it's your spotlight? You will know because when you are in your true spotlight it, doesn't feel like work. It feels different. It makes you feel energized, alive, and glowing.

BUSINESS PLAN FOR LIFE

You may be asking how you can get in touch with your inner voice. If you truly want to get to know yourself, you have to listen to your inner voice and write down what you hear. Writing is priceless to me. It has been the best way for me to get in touch with my inner voice and the dreams in my heart. Although journaling is popular today, I have been writing down my thoughts and feelings for as long as I can remember. When I was young, we called it a diary. It had a tiny lock and key (which was always lost). It was common for girls to write in their diary each night. Boys didn't have the same habit. If you are a man, I am pretty sure you didn't keep a diary in your youth, and the thought of journaling may seem too girly. If so, then think of it as writing a business plan for your life.

Begin by asking yourself a question, listen for the answer and then write it down. Can't think of a question? Then start with this: What do I really love to do? I will list more exploration questions at the end of this chapter.

WRITE IT **ALL** DOWN

Throughout the years, my writing has taken many forms. I write about the events of the day. I write out my prayers, my thoughts and my dreams. I write out my frustration, my fears, and my anger. Through the written word, we can come to real truths and realizations about ourselves. If we get out of the way and just listen to our soul, we will be enlightened.

A few years ago I read a passage in a book that really gave me the freedom to write. This may seem unnecessary, but I feel like I need to tell you what I learned. No one has the right to read your words without your permission. I believe if we think someone else is going to read our deepest thoughts, our silliest dreams we will be cautious about what we write. So, if that is your fear, then make sure you keep your journal, your personal business plan, in a safe place. Give yourself the freedom to be really honest. Be creative and have some fun! Use the written word to express all of your emotions.

When we start a business, buy a house or get a loan, we always put the deal in writing. Yet, we seldom create the most important deal of all, the deal with ourselves. The what must come before the how. Write down what you want and you'll be amazed at what happens. As you begin to write down what you feel you are hearing, it will get easier and it may even be fun.

Take some time and write down these questions in your journal, and immediately write down the answers you hear in your soul. Let your imagination soar! We have to know "what" we want before we can ever figure out "how" to make it happen.

What do I really love to do?

If money were no object what would I be doing?

My biggest dream is...

What is my biggest fear?

Who do I really admire that is living their dreams?

What do I want to be doing ten years from now?

What is my, unique, personal spotlight?

What are my unique qualities?

What shadows do I hide behind?

SPOTLIGHT QUOTE

"It's seizing the day and accepting responsibility for your future. It's seeing what other people don't see, and pursuing that vision no matter who tells you not to."
Howard Schultz, Starbucks

"When the mind talks, the body listens. We literally talk ourselves into and out of every victory or defeat in the game of life."

DR. DENIS WAITLEY

CHAPTER SEVEN

Changing the Energy in the Battery

"The What Must Come Before the How."

"The thoughts that we choose to think are the tools we use to paint the canvas of our lives."

What a powerful statement. Stop right now and reflect on the meaning of this one sentence. Notice it says, "choose to think." That's something that took me years to understand. I didn't realize that I created my reality. The Bible says, "As a man thinketh in his heart, so is he." I thought I was incapable of achieving anything in my life. I lived in the shadows. For many years it was a self-fulfilling prophecy. Once we get ourselves into a situation, we stay in that situation because of our thoughts. We can't get what we "do want" while focusing on what we "don't want." It's very easy to never really take control of our lives because we don't take control of our thoughts.

YOU HAVE CONTROL

If you don't take control of your thoughts, your thoughts will take control of you. We have so much negativity thrown at us, it is up to us to change our thought process. We have to put the screen door on our minds and keep out the things that are not useful in our lives. It's a lesson I continue to learn every day. I know it is our belief systems that set things into motion. I know that disbelief creates an action and brings a result just like belief does. My belief system back in the early 80's told me I would stay in Mississippi so I chose a career that accommodated that belief. As I said earlier, I didn't realize I could leave Mississippi to pursue my dreams. My negative belief system wouldn't allow it.

We must realize that negative beliefs are beliefs, not facts. But those negative beliefs can rob us of the work and the gifts we were sent here to give. We let these negative beliefs create fear and it keeps us paralyzed. Many times it isn't the person with the most talent that succeeds, it is the person who has the strength to look their fear in the face and conquer it. Many times the person who moves to center stage is the one that dared to stare fear in the face and move forward. Fear is such a thief and it will rob you of so many wonderful things if you choose to let it take control.

Somewhere in our lives we have heard and accepted the messages that we are not athletic enough, smart enough, talented enough, pretty enough or wealthy enough to get what we truly want out of life. What we must realize now is that those messages are just words. They become our reality only when we act on them and accept them as truth. Our beliefs become our reality. In my early years, I believed I had nothing to give. I believed that everybody else was talented. (I thought I was behind the door when God was handing out talent in 1959.) I acted on those beliefs for many, many years. I was in my late 20's before I began to take a look at what I believed about myself and what I believed about life. For the first time I looked at myself from the inside out. I finally realized that God had not passed over me. He blessed me with a different kind of gift, one that isn't ordinary or common. I had to begin to change so many things in my life to begin this new journey. I had to change my beliefs, the way I talked to myself and what I expected for my future.

IT ALL COMES BACK

When you think a thought or speak a word, it will come back to you in one way or another. For years, I gave out the wrong thoughts and attitudes. What about you? What is coming back into your world right now? Stop and ask yourself what you have been sending out. If you want to change your life, you must first change your belief system. Your beliefs are what control your thoughts, your thoughts control your actions and your actions control your results. Take a long look at your life and see if your belief systems are keeping you in the shadows. It was my belief system kept me in the shadows for years. If you do not like the events that are happening in your life stop and look at what you believe about yourself and your life. It's a daily journey. If you want to continue to build your belief system I recommend that you read The Magic of Believing by Claude Bristol. This incredible book was written in 1948 but the truth and principles he shares are just as effective today.

FAITH IS TIMELESS

The principles of belief are timeless. The Bible offers story after story about people who were healed because of their beliefs. What are your beliefs about yourself, your health, and your future? Stop right now and give this some thought. You are creating your life by your thoughts and actions. Are you living the life that you want right now? Are you getting the results you want? Belief isn't a one-time decision; it is a daily effort. If you want a nail to go into a piece of wood, you have to hammer it more than once. It is the same with changing your belief system. You must to continue to tap your beliefs into your subconscious mind. You will not get the results you want with just one tap. When you are at a place in your life where nothing seems to be going right, you must take control of your mind and your thoughts.

MIND CONTROL

This game of mind control is not an easy game to play. In fact, it's one of the hardest games you will ever play. It's difficult to stay positive when everything around you seems to be falling apart. It's very hard. That is why very few people do it. I know it is extremely difficult to believe that success is headed your way when you can't even pay your bills. I know how it feels because I have been there. But, if you choose to believe you can't pay your bills, then you won't. Even in the middle of the storm, you must look for the lighthouse. You must believe you will find it. What have you got to lose by changing your thought process? Nothing! But you do have every-thing to gain. Decide what you want. Start with one thing and believe—and I mean really believe—that you can achieve it and then start taking the "action" steps necessary to make it happen.

DO NOT RETURN TO SENDER

When you put your beliefs into operation, people and resources will come your way. Don't send them back. Many times we want things to happen in our life and when it comes to us in an unexpected way, we turn it away. Because it didn't come to us the way we planned, we reject it.

Learning to receive has been a hard lesson for me. I pray, I ask, I believe but I have a hard time receiving. I will give and give of my time, but I am still learning how to receive. I know my difficulty in receiving is a part of my belief system. Somewhere in my past I was taught to give, but I was never taught to receive. I am working to change my belief system about receiving. Do you have trouble receiving? Remember, you reap what you sow in every area of your life including your belief system and your thoughts. What type of thoughts have you been planting? What type of seeds have you been planting? Do you need to pray for a crop failure? Plant good thoughts if you want to have positive results. Try it for 24 hours. Try to only focus on possibility for the next 24 hours. It doesn't mean we won't have problems but we need to stop focusing on the problem and focus on solutions. Be willing to take the first step, regardless of how small it may be, and miracles will happen.

Is it easy for me? No. Does my negative censor sometimes still tell me I can't make it and that I am not good enough? Occasionally. The messages still come; the doubt still creeps in and shows its ugly head. However, I recognize it now but sooner. What I have learned is that the censor only gets stronger when I listen, accept it, and act on it.

POWER YOUR CAR

When you begin to change your belief systems, you must also become responsible for keeping positive power in your soul. It is the negative talk and energy that will send you running back into the shadows. You have to learn how to change the negative energy in your personal batteries to positive energy. How? For many years I depended on others to do it for me. I wanted them to make me happy, change my attitude, and improve my life. I believed if they could see my talent and encourage me, I could make it. It's as if I wanted someone to fill my car with gas *and* pay for it. All I wanted to do was drive. I didn't want any of the personal responsibility. The "gas" I needed in my life was encouragement and approval from others. I thought if I had enough, I would run at one hundred percent. I waited and waited. No matter how much support or encouragement I received, it was never enough.

I began to realize that the only person who can really fuel my tank is me. Each day I have to fill my tank and silence my censor. I have to be responsible for turning the negative energy into positive energy. If I want to produce positive things, I have to put positive things into my spirit. One way I fuel my tank is through affirmations. What are affirmations? Affirmations are positive statements you make about your life and your future. They are your weapons against the shadows of doubt. I post my affirmations on the wall behind my computer so I can see them as I work. I write them in my journal. The more often I say or read my affirmations, the more they become a part of my heart and mind. They are my tools for transforming my soul and my spirit.

BE TRANSFORMED

The Bible tells us to "Be ye transformed by the renewing of your mind." How do you renew your mind? What does the word "renew" mean? It means to energize, to awaken, and to refresh. Transforming your mind can't be done with negative information. When you renew your mind, you find inner peace. When you are at peace, your soul radiates a different kind of energy. When you are at peace, it's easier to deal with anything negative that may occur. When you renew your mind it begins to act as a shield around your soul.

SOUL FOOD

Each day I read uplifting literature to transform my mind. This is the mental food that feeds my mind just like the food that keeps my body alive! The positive, truthful affirmations keep my spirit alive. The more you go within when you are doing without, the stronger you will become. Begin today to honor yourself by listening to YOUR soul, YOUR spirit, and YOUR inner voice. Have the courage to follow its lead. You will be amazed at where it will take you. Your higher power will never give you a dream you don't have the tools to fulfill.

Start building your arsenal of weapons against the shadows of doubt. Write your affirmations down on paper, write them in your calendar, and put them on note cards so you can take them with you each day. We live in a negative world where thinking positive thoughts and making positive statements isn't normal. Affirmations can help change the energy in your internal battery from negative to positive. Affirmations will help you begin to change your world.

Affirmations need to be written in present tense. Don't create your affirmations in future tense such as "I will be a stronger person." Write them in present tense, "I *am* a stronger person." One of the greatest books I've read concerning positive affirmations is called *The Game of Life and How to Play I*, by Florence Scovel Shinn. If you are serious about changing the negative energy in your life, this book should be a part of your personal library. Shinn can help you develop the weapons to wage war on the demons of doubt. It is a truly incredible book.

Here are a few affirmations that can help you begin to change the energy in your soul from negative to positive.

Belief takes you where you want to go. What do you believe about yourself?

Change your inner dialogue with affirmations and you will change your beliefs.

I expect the best.

Champions give their best effort daily. I am a champion.

I realize that stability in my life must come from the inside not the outside.

No matter how it feels, I am moving forward.

I let go in order to receive.

My past does not create my future.

I live my life, not just endure it.

I identify problems and empower solutions.

I work on improving myself everyday.

Everything I need in my life is being sent to me

All things I seek are also seeking me.

Create your own personal affirmations that work for you. It should be something you can remember easily and repeat often.

SPOTLIGHT QUOTE

"We either make ourselves miserable or we make ourselves strong. The amount of work is the same."
Carlos Castenada

"Take chances, make mistakes. That's how you grow. Pain nourishes your courage. You have to fail in order to practice being brave."

MARY TYLER MOORE

CHAPTER EIGHT

The Thief That Robs Us

I believe we continually face an enemy that can rob us of so many things in our life including joy, productivity and satisfaction. What is the thief? FEAR! Teacher and author Pema Chödrön has a wonderful definition of fear. She writes, "Fear is our natural reaction of moving closer to the truth." When we get close to the truth, we begin to be afraid. What happens when something scares us? We usually retreat. We want to hide. Every time you allow fear to dominate and control your life, you are giving up joy and productivity. Fear has a way of sucking the energy and life right out of you. The more you fear something the bigger it gets. It's like a microscope. The more you focus in on an object, the bigger and more powerful it seems. If you just pull back and put your fears into perspective, it will give you new insight. What we focus on multiplies. We must learn to give more power and more focus to our courage, not our fears.

BIGGER THAN THEY SEEM

Many times we wonder why we continue to get what we don't want. I believe it's because that is where we put our focus. We are focused on the problem, the lack of something, the small stuff. Once we get into this cycle, it is hard to break. It takes a strong, brave person to look at their problems and the problems of the world and not become overwhelmed with worry and fear. But how does worry or fear help? When you think about all the things you have feared of or worried about over the years, how many of them came true? Do you remember the things you have been really afraid of in your past? How many of them came true? It's been said that over 90% of the things we fear never come true. We spend energy being fearful when we could be using that energy to look for solutions to our fears.

LET GO AND RECEIVE

Life is about choices. On a day to day basis we have big choices and little choices. Sometimes we have choices between two solutions and we don't like either solution. Regardless of where you are in your life, you have a choice to take action or be motivated by fear. I believe fear appears when we are trying to hang on too tight to someone or something. When are afraid we are losing something, we become fearful and we hold on even tighter. It then becomes a self-fulfilling prophecy and we lose what we so desperately wanted to keep. What do we need to do when the fear is gripping us? What should we do when we are afraid of losing our dreams, our relationships, and our energy? I've seen this so many times in relationships. We become afraid that we are losing this person and we start to be controlling and holding on to tight. It's a natural reaction but we need to just let go and give.

When we are truly afraid we hold on too tight. Try this: Take your hands, put them together and make a tight fist. If I wanted to give you a box stuffed full of a million dollars, what would you have to do to take it from me? You would have to let go and open your hands. So many times we have to let go in order to receive. We have to let go of how we think things should happen. We have to let go of our fear.

FEAR OR FAITH

When you are in the midst of fear, give of yourself. Give more than you think you should and more than you think you can. Amaze others with your spirit of giving. What will happen? By giving, you will be rewarded. Faith is about giving. Fear is about taking. Faith and fear cannot exist at the same time. You have to choose which one you want in your life. Fear creates doubt. One fear feeds the next and before you know it, the problem is out of control.

We have deficient thinking instead of abundance thinking. We don't realize that the more we learn to look at the abundance in our lives, the more abundance we will receive. As we face some of the hardest and most challenging times in our lives, we will learn this lesson over and over again. The things that we need to learn present themselves to us on a daily basis. When we learn the lessons, we can move on.

KEEP GROWING

Every time I think I have my fear under control, something happens that reminds me I don't always practice what I believe. When I feel fear in my relationships, I must walk in quiet faith. When I feel fear in my business, I must walk in quiet faith. I have to walk toward faith and away from fear. You can walk away from the fear that is binding you! Whatever it may be, get strong and stand in the face of fear. If someone or something was threatening your life, or the lives of those you love, you would stand up and fight. Do the same to fear. It is threatening your emotional well being, your spiritual life and your physical life. Do NOT give in. Stand up for yourself. Say in your soul, and in your heart, "Fear, you are not welcome here. I am a creation of the almighty God. You have no power here." Write it down! Say it to yourself! Say it out loud! Believe it and you will see it start to change your life.

We all face different types of fear. We face fear as a nation, as a community, as families, and as individuals. We face situations that buckle us with fear. But we need to step away from the fear and realize the truth. It is the truth that truly will set you free. What truth? Nothing has power over you that you do not give power to. With the help of God, you are in control of your life. Regardless of what your circumstances may be, you give power to either fear or faith. It's hard to stand in the middle of a fearful situation and chose faith when fear seems to be the easy way out. Don't do it! Begin to set yourself apart from others; be a warrior for you. Take charge of your life, shackle your fear with unstoppable FAITH and get out of the shadows. Dance in your own spotlight ! It's waiting for you.

DON'T LET FEAR COST YOU

One of the most important relationships I have in my life is a result of denying my fear, putting aside my ego, listening to direction and writing down what I felt. Many times when we go head to head with fear, it truly seems impossible to conquer. Often, it seems more reasonable to follow what fear is telling us.

I want to share this story with you because it was a great test for me. It tested my ability to stand up to my fear. It tested my ability to resist the opinions of others. It tested my ability to follow my heart and my inner guide.

It began a few years ago when I had the distinct impression I was suppose to contact an old acquaintance. The word impression here is really too mild. I was overwhelmed with the feeling that I was supposed to call him. I didn't know this man very well, but the feeling I should contact him kept hammering at me. I had not seen this person in months. I had no reason to even be thinking about him.

One day while at a speaking engagement, his name and face kept popping into my brain. It seemed so odd to be thinking of him. My ego kicked in full force and I began doubting myself and this urge I had to contact him. What would he think? Would he think I was totally crazy? After several months of arguing with myself and realizing I wasn't following the principles I teach, I contacted him. I'll admit I took the easy way out; I sent a card. If he didn't respond, at least I had taken action. I rationalized that I didn't want to embarrass him, yeah, right, I was trying not to embarrass myself !

But he did respond. He even asked me to lunch and then told me he was going through a very difficult time and needed my friendship. He kept saying, "It's so wild you contacted me." After talking and sharing for many months, we developed a very solid friendship. I knew my presence in his life had helped him through a very difficult time. I was proud of myself for following my inner

SOLO IN THE SPOTLIGHT

voice and not giving into my fear of "looking stupid". I felt like I had done my job and helped a friend in need.

But, my inner voice kept chattering away! In fact, I wanted it to shut up because what it was telling me was scaring me to death!! My inner voice told me this man would be my husband. It was a ridiculous idea. It couldn't happen. He was one of ex-husband's best friends. He was recently divorced. He was seeing someone! My list of why it couldn't work went on and on.

Years before this relationship began, I had spent time writing down all the things I wanted in a relationship. I also wrote down the characteristics I wanted in the man I would one day marry. The more I got to know Rob, the more I realized he was the man I had described in my journal. Wow! I couldn't believe I was falling for him. It didn't make sense. However, I decided to let go of my fears and doubts and see what would happen. There were days when my friends told me to give up on the relationship. They told me they were afraid I was going to be devastated. But, I listened to my heart and my soul. It took a number of years, and a long walk of faith, but as I sit here and write these words, Rob is now my husband. Why? Because I took a leap of faith. I listened to my inner voice. I faced my fears.

Every time I look at him, I realize that fear almost cost me one of the most precious relationships in my life. He has thanked me over and over again for listening to my heart and for taking the risk to act on that voice. He has thanked me for not giving into the voice of fear or the opinions of others.

JUST DO IT

If you are feeling the urge to call someone, take a risk and do it. Ask yourself what is the worst thing that could happen? Usually it's the fear of rejection that keeps us from following that voice from within. Think about what you could possibly gain by taking the risk. So whatever your heart is saying to you right now, take action.

Listen and trust your heart and soul. Take a leap of faith; you'll be ecstatic that you did.

Whatever you truly believe you can do, begin it now. I believe the key to dealing with fear is to NOT bail out when it gets tough. We have to stay in there, keep exploring and keep taking risks. Fear will never leave our lives if we continue to push ourselves to grow. It's not about eliminating fear from our lives; it's learning to grow through the fear. It's learning to take action in spite of the fear. Remember, action has magic, grace and power in it! Take it from someone who knows. Be brave and look your fears in the face!

—— Success Work ——

What have you been fearful of in the past? How did you face it?

What has fear cost you?

How do you react to fear?

What is your biggest fear?

What actions can you now take when you are faced with fear?

What inner dialogue do you hear when you are faced with fear?

SPOTLIGHT QUOTE
"Fear is that little darkroom where negatives are developed."
Michael Pritchard

"Hang in there. Many of life's failures are people who did not realize how close they were to success when they gave up."

THOMAS EDISON

CHAPTER NINE

Pushing Past the Limits of Your Mind

After we identify our fears, we can't just sit back and wait, saying, "I'm not afraid anymore. I can just wait for something to happen." No, the fun has just begun! After we have identified our shadows and faced our fears, we have to learn the tools that will keep us forever in that light.

Your limits will be tested over and over again. The question is, will you push yourself to a new level or will you coast? The true winners in life are willing to sweat out that extra mile, put in that extra hour, and make that extra call to find their success. Other people can push you but you have to decide whether YOU want it or not. It's up to you to get out of your "comfort" zone. When I am at the gym working out, my workout partner can push me to lift a heavier weight, but there is NOTHING she can do if I refuse to participate. I have to pick up the weight. It wouldn't matter what was said to me, I have to make the decision to participate and push myself.

There are many times we have to push our personal limits. We have to push ourselves to watch what we eat and drink, to make sure we get enough sleep and the right amount of exercise. However, the biggest thing we have to push through is the limit in our own mind. We have to be the watchmen at the gate of our own world. We have to be the David to the Goliath in our own minds. Most of the time the thing that defeats us is the fear and doubt we keep around us day in and day out. The success and happiness you experience in your life depends on the watchmen at the gate of your thoughts. If you allow negative thoughts to enter, sooner or later those thoughts will crystallize and begin to produce external results. You can be a giant in your world when you begin to stop the negative assault on your own future. Many times we would never allow another person to verbally assault us the way we assault ourselves. We nourish negative thoughts by giving them attention. The negative thoughts begin to grow and become stronger. Wherever you put your attention and focus, it becomes stronger and takes a strong hold in your world.

FIRE WALKING

Several years ago I attended a seminar in Florida given by a very well known motivational speaker. I have admired him for years. I have watched with interest as he has helped millions of people through his CD's and books. My son Nick even knows him thanks to his appearance in "Shallow Hal."

The seminar I attended was the famous "fire walk" seminar. The "mission" was to give participants the tools to face their fear and have the confidence to walk across beds of hot coals. I'll be really honest, walking on hot coals has never been on my list of goals or on my "to do" list. I have way too many pairs of high heels to take the chance of never wearing any of those shoes again. If I am going to have blisters on my feet, it's going to be from a pair of brand new four-inch heels. I loved the seminar but when it came time to walk those coals, I decided not to do it. I wasn't afraid. I simply didn't need prove to myself that I could do it. I watched over 1500 people walk the coals including several of my closest friends. It actually was totally fascinating to see all of these fire pits with people walking across the coals at 1:00 in the morning. What I realized is what Zen Master Ling Chi said is true, "The miracle is not to walk on burning coals or in the thin air or on the water; the miracle is to walk on the earth." Each day we are alive and breathing and living is another miracle. I didn't need to push myself to walk on hot coals. I have a different kind of "fire walk". I need to push myself in other areas. I know I need to push myself into making time to get quiet with myself, listen and write. I need to push myself each day to be creative. My fire walk is a day to day journey to step outside of my comfort zone and grow and change.

POISON OR POWER

There are times I look around and wonder why more people are not stepping out and stretching themselves to a new level. Why aren't they pushing to maximize their inner strengths and talents? I believe that one reason we do NOT push past the limits in our mind is because of the internal dialogue that continues to play inside our heads. We have touched on this in other chapters, but I want to take it one more step and show you how you are creating either poison or power in your life.

Remember this old adage? "Sticks and stones may break my bones, but words will never hurt me." How many times have these words been chanted on a school playground? I can just hear children saying it in a singsong rhyme filled will sarcasm. Cute, freckled faced little girls singing those words to rowdy little boys. We sang that rhyme as a child, and yet the words did hurt. Often, the most pain we can cause someone is through our words. In fact, the times I have been brought to my knees were from someone's hurtful, poisonous, powerful words. Yes, I am sure many people have experienced horrific physical pain. I've had my share. I have broken both of my elbows at the same time, my nose has been broken twice and I have had major surgery more than once. But, I don't really remember what the pain felt like. I know it wasn't pleasant but when I try and remember it I can't feel the physical pain of the past. However, when I recall times when I was verbally assaulted, I immediately remember how it felt. I can feel the sick feeling the emotional turmoil, and the darkness that surrounded the experience.

All words can be poison or power, darkness or light, courage or fear, a blessing or a curse. Words can start wars and end wars. They start relationships and end relationships. God began the creation of the world by using these words, "Let there be light." However, many of us never think about the world we are creating with the words we use each day. We just talk and talk and wonder why our lives end up the way that they do.

THINKING IN PICTURES

It doesn't matter if its words we speak to ourselves or words spoken to us by someone else, all words create word pictures. How many times have someone's words played over and over in your mind? Maybe you hear them over and over again because they bring you joy. But, how many times do you punch the replay button on those hurtful, dream-stealing, emotion-draining words someone has said to you? When you do, you instantly feel the emotional pain all over again.

The Bible says, "No word returns to us void." If we truly believed the statement, wouldn't we change the things we say to ourselves and to others? What if every word you said had a physical manifestation? For example, if you say, "I will never make that sale," you suddenly get a call from the client who tells you the deal is off. What if you say, "I think my kids are coming down with a cold" and within an hour they are sick? What if every word you spoke instantly came true wouldn't you be more cautious about what you say?

The words you use create your world. When you speak, you are spreading poison or power to your soul, spirit and into your physical world. It's time to stop the verbal assault on ourselves and start creating the world we want.

Our mind is the master designer of our inner qualities and our outer circumstances. Our thoughts determine our actions and our fate. We are always the masters of our own world, even when we are in our weakest state. We are still the only person in charge of ourselves.

I ask my seminar participants to begin to change the words they use each day. Think about some of the phrases we use on a regular basis. For example, "I am freezing to death," "I am scared to death," "I am working myself to death," "Those kids are driving me crazy," or "I'm about to pull my hair out." What if every word we spoke came true? Can you imagine walking through a crowded airport or hotel? We would see people frozen solid in blocks of ice, people without any hair, and people going crazy. People would drop dead left and right!

TRANSFORMING YOUR WORLD

I truly believe you can transform your world if you will transform the way you talk to yourself and others. I teach my audiences to replace the negative, energy-draining words with positive words. If you are constantly telling other people you are stressed out your mind goes to work to make this a reality. Your body simply follows the directions of your mind. The next time you catch yourself starting to say you are stressed out change it to, "I am blessed out."

If you woke up above ground today without a chalk line around your body, YOU ARE BLESSED! If you are capable of reading these words, you are blessed. Look around at your blessings right now! How would your life change if you made the choice to always look for your blessings? Stop saying you are stressed and be blessed! ! It all begins with the words you say and think. Change the phrase, "I am so nervous" to "I am energized." If you talk about being nervous then your body follows that mental command and you begin to act nervous. If you are going into a job interview and you constantly talk about being nervous before you go into the interview that is the energy you take in the room with you. Choose to take energy with you and not nervousness. When we are overworked and have too much to do we many times talk about being "overwhelmed". That one statement feels heavy and unbearable. When you begin to feel overwhelmed simply change the statement to "in demand." If we are going to push ourselves and achieve more then we will be in demand. You feel more important if you are in demand. You can begin to change your attitude, your actions, and your world if you begin to take control of your thoughts and words.

Is it easy to change the way you talk and think, NO! It is the hardest thing you will ever do. I teach this everyday and it's hard to practice. A few years ago I was getting ready for a speaking engagement and Nick was driving me nuts. I was practicing everything I just told you not to do. I finally looked at him and through clinched teeth I said, "Nick, you better get out of my kitchen and stop driving me crazy." Nick looked at me with love in his eyes and said so sweetly, "Mom, you don't have to let my actions affect your attitude." I almost passed out. I couldn't believe my 10 year old was giving me an attitude adjustment. I told him to stop listening to my CD's but then hugged him and thanked him for the Life Lesson! Remember that, "You don't have to let anyone's actions affect your attitude." Powerful !!!

Transformation to an improved life begins from within. It truly is a journey into "inner space." I know that you have places in your life that you need to stretch, grow and push yourself. Take some time and think about the following thoughts. Take inventory of where you are.

——— *Success Work* ———

What areas of your life do you need to get out of your comfort zone?

Where do you need to push yourself?

What "negative words" are a part of your daily life that you can change?

What words do you need to transform to change your attitude?

Make it your goal to speak positively for the next 24 hours. If you find yourself not meeting your goal then the 24 hours start over.

SPOTLIGHT QUOTE
"Talk back to your internal critic."
Robert McKain

"The secret of making something work in your lives is, first of all, the deep desire to make it work: then the faith and belief that it can work: then to hold that clear definite vision in your consciousness and see it working out step by step, without one thought of doubt or disbelief."

EILEEN CADDY

CHAPTER
TEN

If You Believe It, Then You Will See It

WHAT'S YOUR DREAM?

I have always loved the quote from the movie *Field of Dreams*, "Build it and they will come". I feel that one simple statement describes exactly what we must do if we want our goals and dreams to become a reality. We have to build the dream, create the dream and then the evidence of that dream will show up in our lives. Earlier we talked about discovering our passion and finding the things we really love to do. Now is the time to begin to turn those thoughts into reality. I grew up on a farm in Mississippi and experienced the principle of sowing and reaping. I believe our dreams work on that same type of universal principle. We have to plant those dreams like seeds deep in our soul and then we have to maintain them. I believe one of the first steps to planting your dreams is to write those dreams down. . It plants the dream in your heart and soul and you see the evidence on paper. Have you written down one goal or one dream? If not, why not? If you haven't, turn to the back of this book and DO IT NOW ! It can be anything you want it to be. Remember this is YOUR dream, your spotlight that you are creating. Dreams aren't what someone has told you should do. Dreams are what you want to do. Have the courage to write down whatever is popping into your brain right now.

BRIGHT LIGHTS

I spend a great deal of time writing down my goals and dreams. I don't write them down once I write them down daily and I suggest you do the same thing. It helps anchor them in our soul. Several years ago I really wanted to do a television show. I wanted to fulfill that dream but I was afraid to even write it down. It seemed so crazy. I wasn't famous and I didn't believe there was a possibility that I could secure something on television. After arguing with myself I finally "wrote it down." It was in tiny, little print but I wrote it down. Two weeks after I wrote that goal down I received a phone call from someone I really didn't know asking me to host a music talent show. I told her I was available and I would love to do it. As we finished the conversation she said, " Oh, did I mention they will be filming this for television? They are hoping to syndicate the show." I couldn't believe it !! I had only written the goal down 2 weeks before that phone call. We filmed that show and the next year I hosted it with Dick Clark. It was a lesson for me. I have continued to be more specific with my "television" dream and as you are reading this I am being considered to host a national talk show and I have my own segment on a television show in Nashville on our NBC affiliate. It works. It truly works !!! Don't negotiate with yourself, write it down !!!!!!!!!!!!

INTERNAL VISION

Unfortunately, just having a goal or dream is not enough. They require work. Think about your dream as you would planting a seed. When a seed is planted no one knows it's there but you. You planted it and you water it. Eventually the seed grows and pops up through the earth. Then it requires daily maintenance. You have to water your dream seed even when it's still in the dark. I believe that is why it's important to write it down. We have to do the maintenance on these dreams. You have to believe that if you maintain it on a daily basis it will push its way out of the dark and into the light. Just because no one else can see your dream seed doesn't mean it's not growing. We have to see with an inner eye, hear with an inner ear.

GO WITHIN

Once your dreams slowly emerge into the light, it takes a different kind of maintenance. If you are a songwriter, you have to keep writing. If you are a singer searching for a record deal, you have to keep pitching your demo. If you are in sales, you have to keep making the calls. If you are an actor, you have to keep going to auditions. You have to do the work to feed and nurture your dream. You must do whatever it takes to make it happen.

Even when your dream can't be seen by others, you are growing and improving yourself. Then it happens. The phone rings and you suddenly have six songs on the next Garth Brooks album. (I have a friend who got that call!) You don't know the day or the hour when the tide will turn. Maybe you're in network marketing and you've shared the business idea over and over. Finally, someone understands and your dream becomes a reality. Maybe you have a manuscript you have submitted over and over again. Keep submitting it. My friend, author Mark Victor Hansen was rejected over and over again with his book, *Chicken Soup for the Soul.* Mark never gave up and now it has sold over sixty million copies. Maybe your dream isn't for success in business. Maybe you dream of a special relationship you know you are supposed to have. Keep loving and giving unconditionally and one day your partner will see the light, too. We must learn to walk in quiet confidence. We have to go within and find our strength even when we are doing without.

As your dream develops, you have to rely on never-ending faith. How do you obtain never-ending faith? By practicing the principles in this book. You change the way you talk, you write down your vision, you create a plan and you refer to it often. Read examples of people who have gone against the odds and made it. It will renew your faith. You must be able to see that dream in your minds eye before anyone else will ever see it.

 One of my favorite stories is about Epcot Center in Florida. Roy Disney, Walt Disney's brother, was on hand for opening day. A reporter said to Roy, " This must be a bittersweet day for you. You must be thrilled that Walt's dream has come true but you must be really sad that Walt never got to see it." Without hesitation Roy Disney replied, " That's where you are wrong Walt DID see it. That's why YOU get to see it." Now an entire economy in central Florida is based on one man's dream. Walt Disney saw it in his heart and soul before anyone else saw it. It is the same with you. YOU have to see it first.

BELIEVE IT BEFORE YOU SEE IT

Another great example of following a dream is the story of Noah. Can you imagine the faith Noah had to have to build an ark? He didn't live close to any water! Imagine the criticism Noah received from those around him. But, Noah acted on faith. He began building the ark before it started raining. He had a plan that God had given him and he followed it. He learned how to listen. We have to keep building our ark just like Noah did even when no one else can see it. Noah drew a picture of the ark long before he built it. He knew what the ark would look like and he just kept building. Our dreams are our ark. Many times it takes years for us to build it and many times everyone around us thinks we are crazy. But, when we know what our passion and our purpose is, we will keep building the ark even when it's not raining. Can you imagine the faith that it took Noah? Do you have that kind of faith to keep building and keep believing that there is a purpose for this dream that you have been given? Why would you give up now?

It wasn't raining when Noah built the ark. If he had waited for the rain he would have drowned with everyone else. We have to follow our dreams even when it seems weird or stupid and NO ONE else can see it. It only matters that you can see it. Les Brown says, "What someone thinks about your dream is none of your business." This is your business and you better make it your business to stay close to your dream in your spirit. You better have a vision and a picture of your ark. Noah had a plan. Do you? You can't build an ark without a plan! What is your dream? Start building it now. Build it now and it will come.

You have to keep building the dream that is inside you that gives you passion and sets your soul on fire. You have to have the faith and determination of Noah. Remember, Noah was seven hundred years old when he began building the ark. You have much more of an advantage than that!

CREATE YOUR DREAM BOOK

How do you water the dream when it's still just an idea? I will tell you what I do. Since we think in pictures not in words, I created a Dream Book. It is a three ring binder full of pictures of my dreams and goals. I take time to cut out pictures out of magazines. I cut out words and phrases. On the front of my Dream Book are all the words of a Dreamer. I look at it often. I have a picture of huge seminars with thousands of people attending because that is one of my dreams. I have a picture of Oprah because my goal is to be on her show. I have a picture of the car I want to drive. I have photos of the cities and countries I want to visit. I have so much fun with this book.

In the back of this book are instructions on how to create your own Dream Book. I urge you to create one for yourself. Then encourage your spouse and children to create one, too. You could create a family dream book and let everyone add their dream to the book. I have taught my son Nick to dream and set goals to reach those dreams since he was very little. We would go out and dream build. It has been a wonderful time for us to spend together.

GET RID OF THE WEEDS

As your dream begins to grow and it begins to see the light of day, you must be your own dream gardener. Once your dream starts taking shape, it requires a different type of care. You still have to water the dream, but now you also have to keep the weeds out. You have to be your own personal weed eater. Those weeds are walking around disguised as human beings. They see your dream starting to grow. They tell you why it will never be more than a dream. They are Dream Stealers. You can recognize them by their words such as, "Don't get your hopes up too high," "Be careful," or "Don't take that risk." Battling with a Dream Stealer is one of the hardest battles you will ever fight. Dreams are like infants. You would never expose a newborn baby to someone that is sick. You protect that baby. Your dreams are your baby. Protect them and nourish them and don't expose them to someone that will try and infect them with fear and doubt.

STRONGER THAN THE WIND

When friends or family do not support your dreams, you have to make some big decisions. Do you follow the dream in your heart or do you allow someone to steal that dream? You must walk on in quiet confidence. J. W. Marriott said, " Good timber does not grow with ease. The stronger the wind, the stronger the trees." Your dreams are trees that grow stronger in the wind. When the wind of doubt and disbelief begins to blow around you remember you have roots that are anchored in faith! They may blow your dreams from side to side but you won't be uprooted! Stand tall and stand strong! You can listen to those whose judgment you trust and see if their objections are valid. But, truly, in the end you must follow your voice wherever it may lead. You must fly solo and into your personal spotlight.

FAITH AND FEAR

Flying solo requires a combination of faith and fear. It is natural that stepping out on our own, admitting our dreams and writing them down is frightening. But if we truly understand Denis Waitley's idea that fear is false evidence appearing real, then we must understand that faith is finding answers in the heart. It's what we must rely on when it comes time to take that solo flight. Maybe it means finally following your heart and pursuing the career that has been calling you. It may not be practical, but your heart sings when you think of it. Maybe it means going back to school or ending an unhealthy relationship. Whatever your solo journey, you are the only one that can make it happen. No one else can sing the songs you were meant to sing. No one else can write the words you were sent here to write. No one else can teach the things you were sent here to teach. Your spotlight belongs only to you. It's not about money, or status it's about following your hearts desire.

STAND ALONE

Realize that we each have a solo mission and a solo gift that we are sent here on this earth to share. We have become a nation that is afraid of standing alone. We give up our dreams and heart's desire because someone convinced us that we should follow the crowd. Children believe they can do anything. Just ask them, they will tell you. My son has had dreams of being everything from a woodcutter to a doctor and everything in between. I believe we, as parents, need to listen to the voices of these little ones and hear what they are saying. If they tell you they want to be an astronaut, don't tell them they should be more practical. Encourage them to follow the road less traveled. We teach them not to give into peer pressure and do what is right, yet we steal their dreams by limiting them and forcing them to be realistic. Teach your children by example how to be a Dreamer and Achiever. Help them create their own Dream Book. Encourage them to find their inner voice and how to follow it. Teach them the powerful words of Woody Allen, "Eighty percent of success is showing up." Teach yourself and those around you how to show up with their DREAMS and GOALS! It is the greatest gift you can give them.

Encourage those around you to follow their dreams. Do the same for yourself. Give them their wings. Give yourself wings and fly solo! Get your dreams on paper and do it NOW !

What goals do you want to achieve in the next week, month, or year?

Write down the specific things you want to achieve.

Write down the action steps necessary for you to achieve these goals.

Who discourages your dreams?

Who will support your dreams?

Write yourself a letter as if you were writing it on the last day of this year and tell yourself all the great things you accomplished this past year. Write down every exciting detail. Make two copies of this letter. Mail one copy to one of your dream partners and keep the other one in a place where you can open it on the last day of the year. Get creative.

Create your Dream Book! Have fun and be a kid again!

SPOTLIGHT QUOTE

"To accomplish great things we must not only act, but also dream. Not only plan, but also believe."

Anatole France

"I will persist until I succeed. Always will I take another step. If that is of no avail I will take another, and yet another. In truth, one step at a time is not too difficult... I know that small attempts, repeated, will complete any undertaking."

OG MANDINO

CHAPTER ELEVEN

You Should Just Ask!

We have gone through all the steps of getting our dreams down in writing, of taking control of the negative chatter in our minds, and of being careful about sharing our dreams with Dream Stealers. What do we do now to get our dreams to the next level? We are so much closer to our spotlight because every step we have taken has taken us further away from our shadows of doubt, fear and disbelief. It's time to take that leap of faith and just start ASKING! If we want to achieve our goals, our dreams, follow our passion, we have to start asking. We have to ask God, ask ourselves, ask other people and we have to keep on asking!

BE LIKE A CHILD AGAIN

Do you know what the word NO has always meant to my child? It means ask again. It means keep on asking but ask in a different way. Children know the keys to asking! You must ask Clearly, Confidently, Consistently and Creatively! If you have children, you know what I mean! They are so persistent. They are willing to take risks and keep asking for what they want. They hear the word NO and yet they move forward.

One of the greatest lessons I learned about asking was from Nick. He was about 10 years old and was asking us for a dirt bike for his birthday. I had told him NO at least 100 times. He created a dream book, he wrote his goal list and on that list about 50 times he wrote "dirt bike." He took every principle I teach and used it against me. This went on for about 6 months.

NEW WAY TO ASK

I took Nick with me to a big speaking engagement in Memphis later that same year. I was speaking for a huge network marketing group and on Sunday morning they had a church service for anyone that wanted to attend. The service that day was the Passion Play.

It was a huge production of the Bible from the birth of Jesus to the resurrection. Nick was sitting down front with me fascinated with the live animals and the magnitude of this production. He was listening and his eyes ere huge. In one portion of the play Jesus stepped out to the edge of the stage and held out his arms toward the audience and stated, " You can have anything if you will just ask it in my name." My 10 year old hit his feet and threw his arms toward Jesus and screamed at the top of his lungs, "Dear Jesus, please let my momma and daddy get me a motorcycle for Christmas, Thank You, AMEN!" After I recovered from the shock I grabbed him by the collar of his shirt and yanked him to his seat and told him to sit down and be quiet. Everyone around me is laughing out loud and just shaking their head. Nick didn't miss a beat. He looked up at me and said, "Mom, Jesus said anything." Guess what Nick got for Christmas? Of course, a dirt bike. He found a new way to ask. The faith and determination of a child.

What would your life be like if you adopted the tenacity of a child? As adults, we often take the word "no" so personally. We take it as a personal assault and it shuts us down. We allow fear to creep in. We stop asking because of the pain of rejection. We have to continue to ask if we want to achieve success. If you are in sales, what do you have to do to get the sale? ASK! If you want to spend your life with a partner, what do you have to do? ASK ! If you want to get your song recorded, or your book published, what do you have to do? ASK ! Ask and keep on asking.

My company, Winners By Choice, has created a Goal Card that will remind you to ASK. What does the word ASK mean? Look at it this way:

A – Ask and it shall be given

S – Seek and you will find

K- Knock and the door will be open!

Just ASK! Please log on to our website, *www. WinnersByChoice.com* if you want to be part of the Goal Club and receive your own Goal Card.

I believe the universe rewards us for taking risks. It wasn't a big risk for me to write down my television dream, but it was still a risk. Would my television dream have happened if I had not written it down? I do not know, but I wrote it down and it came true. It was a bigger risk for me to believe that a man I knew only casually would eventually be my husband. I believe God always answers our prayers, but sometimes not the way we want it answered. I think He delivers our request right back into our own hands and then it's up to us to move forward. We have to put our faith into action. What dream is chasing you right now? Stop running. Turn around, face it and surrender to it. Turn to the back of this book and write it down. I dare you! I dare you to dream your dream in writing. Release it from your captive mind and give it the room it needs to soar! Set it free. Set yourself free. Give your dream the wings to fly. When you write it down, it will give you such a sense of relief and joy! Write it down and forget it for a little while. Once you get it outside of your mind, your direction will come if you listen with an open heart and mind.

As I mentioned, I had written down the characteristics I had wanted in a husband long before I met Rob. In this same dream and miracle journal I had written down about thirty other goals. Some of these goals were very simple and some were very serious. When I re-read the journal recently, I discovered I had met all my goals but one. You have in your hands the result of reaching my last goal, a book!

"Ask and it shall be given, seek and you will find, knock and the door will be open." Those are the words from the book of Matthew. Many times we don't get what we want because we just don't know how to ask and we don't keep asking.

The ability to ask comes from developing the inner strength to believe that we deserve something great to happen in our lives. Many times we don't believe we deserve the best , so we never ask for the best. We settle for whatever life throws our way.

CAN I TAKE YOUR ORDER?

Think about every time you go to a restaurant to have a meal. What is the first thing the waiter or waitress asks? "Can I take your order please?" You have to tell them what you want if you want to eat.

I believe life is exactly the same way. We have to ask and we have to be specific! Many people say, "I just want to be happy." Well, what does "happy" look and feel like to you? Describe it. We want our relationships to be fulfilling and happy yet we expect the other person to figure out what we want. You will never have what you truly want in a relationship if you do not ASK for it.

Life is about asking ourselves a series of questions. It's about asking those around us that we share our lives with a series of questions. Ask them if you are meeting their needs. If someone is treating you in a way that makes you uncomfortable, ask them to change their behavior. You have the right to ask.

ASK THE TOUGH QUESTIONS

We need to ask for what we want in life and what we deserve. We need to ask ourselves and we need to ask for it from others. There are some other questions we need to also ask. We will face situations in our lives that are difficult and painful. I know I have. It's the questions we ask ourselves at these crucial times that determine how we grow and rebound from them. When we have been betrayed by a friend, lost a job, or been hurt by a family member, it is easy ask WHY it happened. When we start to ask why ,we miss a real opportunity for growth. Stop asking why and start asking WHAT! When you are having a challenging day, stop and ask these three questions:

1. What am I learning today?
2. What is positive about this situation?
3. How am I growing today?

Change is about letting go. You can't grow if you don't let go.

When we ask why something is happening to us, we develop the victim mentality that takes our power away. When you allow yourself to become a victim, you lose control of your life and you begin to play the blame game. Blame will never take you to your desired destination.

So start ASKING! Ask and keep on asking. Many times we have not because we ask not. What haven't YOU asked for in your life?

Spend some time asking yourself the following questions.

Success Work

What do I need to ask for in my life?

Who do I need to ask for help in my career?

Who can I learn from? Who can I mentor?

What do I need to ask of myself?

What lessons do I need to learn from the difficult situations I have faced?

Remember to ASK:
    Clearly
    Confidently
    Consistently
    Creatively

SPOTLIGHT QUOTE

"Dreams come true when desire transforms them into concrete action. Ask life for great gifts and you encourage life to deliver them to you."
Napoleon Hill

"When I stand before God at the end of my life, I would hope that I would not have a single bit of talent left, and could say, 'I used everything you gave me"

Erma Bombeck

CHAPTER TWELVE

Dance with Destiny

I mentioned in an earlier chapter about my best friend and piano teacher, Cheryl Prewitt. As you recall, she was told she would never walk again but her faith brought her through. She not only walked, but went on to walk the runway in Atlanta City as Miss America! It took her five years to get to her spotlight, but she finally won Miss America.

I began working for her just after she completed her year as Miss America. Cheryl was a Contemporary Christian artist and speaker. I was absolutely sure I had found my spotlight in life by supporting someone who was a star. Because I didn't believe in myself and was still walking in the shadows, I thought the only thing I could do was be a support person. Don't get me wrong, I enjoyed the work, but I hadn't found my spotlight. I realize now that nothing really grows in the shadows. Talents do not grow if you are hiding in a shadow.

I will never forget one of Cheryl's singing engagements that would be life changing for me. We were booked for a large convention in Charlotte, North Carolina. The client had sent his private jet for us. Wow! Here were two country girls from the back roads of Mississippi flying on a private jet! The coliseum was unbelievable. I had never seen a place that big. The stage was huge and lit by an incredible spotlight. Cheryl went backstage to prepare to sing and I went to set up the book and tape table. I remember secretly standing in the upper deck of the coliseum watching Cheryl sing, speak and touch the hearts of 10,000 people. I remember saying to myself, "I will never be able to make a difference in the lives of so many people but I get to work for someone who does." As I stood in that shadow that first dream began to take shape in my heart but my fear didn't allow me to even recognize it.

I slowly walked back to the book and tape table. Audience members were beginning to gather at the table to purchase Cheryl's products and get her picture. Because our features were similar, some people thought I was Cheryl and asked for an autograph. I just smiled and said, "No, I'm not Cheryl. I am Dale, her assistant." Several people still wanted me to sign her name. I was thrilled. I didn't care it wasn't me they wanted. I was happy to be associated with someone who had made such a difference in their lives.

SECRET DREAM

I secretly dreamed at that moment that one day someone would ask me for my autograph. But I knew it would never happen. I would never be a star, but I was happy to work for someone who was.

My experience in Charlotte brought my dream of being on stage to the surface. I remember how strong the desire was in my heart to make a difference doing something I truly loved to do. I didn't verbalize it or share it with anyone, but the dream was ready to grow. Even though Cheryl and I were as close as sisters, I never shared that dream with her. I never shared it with anyone because I knew it was pointless to do so. What could I do? I didn't have a talent that would put me in the spotlight. As I packed up the table that night, I was both sad and happy. I was really thankful that I had been given the opportunity to get this close to my dream of "being somebody". I didn't believe I could ever live that dream but I could work for someone who was!

I realize now that being Cheryl's assistant was safe for me. I could get close to my dream without having to take the risk. I would never have to face the fear of failure or rejection. I could safely stay in the shadows. I could hear the voice inside me, but I pushed it away as childish dreams and fantasy. I know now that every person on this earth has an inner dream. The dream can only begin to unfold when we find the courage to admit what it is. When we finally stand face-to-face with our personal dream, I think God and the universe says, "Yes! Now we can go to work." It took over ten years for that to take place in my life.

BACK IN THE SHADOWS

My experience in Charlotte happened in 1983. In 1994, I was back in a convention hall similar to the Charlotte Coliseum. Once again I was standing in the upper deck watching 15,000 people cheer for the entertainment on stage. I had listened to the speakers; I had watched the entertainers. As I stood in the shadows and listened, I was suddenly transported back to that that night in Charlotte. I remembered everything I had felt that night, the secret desire to be on that stage and the empty feeling I had because the dream would never become a reality.

DREAM SPOTLIGHT

As I slipped down the stairs and into the shadows back stage, I watched as the crowd stood on their feet and began to cheer. I reached up and brushed a tear away because I was now living *my* dream. The crowd was cheering because my name had just been announced as their next speaker. As I walked onto that huge stage and stepped into that incredible spotlight, I looked out across that arena and realized had far I had come. As I looked into the crowd, I wondered who was out there in those shadows with a secret dream just waiting to grow. I said a prayer of thanks that God had gently reminded me of that night in Charlotte. I still marveled at the wonder of it all.

Not only was I speaking to over 15,000 people but I was also sharing the stage with my heroes. For years, I had admired Zig Ziglar and Denis Waitley. They were my heroes long before I ever dared to follow my dream. In recent years, I had fallen in love with Les Brown and his message. When I had arrived at the convention, I was overwhelmed when I found out I was sharing the program with these great gentlemen. That little girl from Mississippi was stepping into the spotlight with her heroes!

DANCE WITH DESTINY

Later that day, I greeted people at my book and tape table. This time the crowd was waiting for me! I can't describe the feelings I had signing my own name. As my convention host escorted me back to the limo to take me back to the hotel, I laid my head back and silently said a prayer of thanks to God. Even if no one else had heard my dream that day in Charlotte, He had. And when I finally had the heart and the courage to admit my secret dream, I walked out of the shadows and into my own personal spotlight.

There is a place for you. There is a spotlight for you. It doesn't matter how old you are or where you are in your life. It's never too late to begin. I started a new career at age 30. Don't let you fear and excuses keep you in the shadows of your life any longer. You can step into your spotlight even if it is one inch at a time. Look inside your soul and begin to turn the light on. You have to turn the light on from within. Listen to that guiding voice and take the chance. Take that leap of faith! The world needs what you and only you have to give.

Your spotlight is waiting for you. It's time for you to get out of the shadows and dance in your own personal spotlight. It's your date and your dance with destiny. I promise you, it's a dance you don't want to miss.

SPOTLIGHT QUOTE

"If you are willing to be the person that you were meant to be, I think you will discover that for you the sky is the limit"

Ted Engstrom

115

I found the following poem as I was doing the final edit for this book. It really shared all of my feelings and my hopes and prayers for each one of you that has shared this time with me. Thank you for helping make my dreams come true by reading this book.

God Bless You!
Dale Smith Thomas

Believe in your Dreams.
Believe in Today.
Believe that you are loved.
Believe that you make a difference.
Believe we can build a better world.
Believe when others might not.
Believe there's light at the end of the tunnel.
Believe that you may be that light for someone else.
Believe that the best is yet to be.
Believe in yourself.
I Believe In You!

KOBI YAMADA

DREAM BOOK EXERCISE

What you will need:
3 Ring Binder
Clear Sheet Protectors
Colored Construction Paper
Magazines
Scissors
Glue
Big Imagination

Fill the 3 ring binder with the sheet protectors. Cut out words, pictures and phrases that describe you and your dreams. Glue these onto the construction paper and fill you DREAM BOOK !

Letting Go Exercise
Write down all the things in your life that you need to let go of. Write down the negative habits, your fears, destructive relationships and anything that is holding you back. After you have written them all down then rip them into small pieces. This is the garbage of your life. Hold all of this garbage in your hands and take it to the trash can and as you dump it into the trash say out loud, " I Release It." Your emotional trash is now in the garbage. Take the garbage out and do not go digging around in the garbage can again. If you feel those old habits starting to enter your life remind yourself you no longer have them, they are in the trash of your past !

ABOUT THE AUTHOR

Dale Smith Thomas is an international professional speaker and author that makes her home in Brentwood, Tennessee. Dale feels that her life's work is to empower others to do more, be more and achieve more. Her dynamic programs have inspired and challenged hundreds of thousands of people to search for their unlimited potential. Dale and her husband Rob live with their family just outside of Nashville, Tennessee.

Dale Smith Thomas
1-888-U2 DREAM
www.WinnersByChoice.com